DASH DONE SLOW

DASH DONE SLOW

The DASH Diet Slow Cooker Cookbook

KAREN FRAZIER

ROCKRIDGE
PRESS

Contents

Introduction

Making a dietary change can feel daunting, particularly if it's a complete overhaul of how you've eaten in the past. Many people, when they hear the words "DASH diet" (or any other "healthy" diet, for that matter), think of flavorless, bland, dry foods. They imagine they'll have to spend hours in the kitchen cooking foods from scratch using hard-to-find ingredients—or eating the same handful of boring meals over and over again. The thought of completely changing everything feels more than challenging; it may even feel impossible.

That's why this slow cooker cookbook was written. It is designed to follow the principles of the DASH diet while providing delicious, interesting, easy-to-prepare meals that will leave you feeling satisfied. Each recipe requires 10 or fewer ingredients (plus salt and pepper) and 15 minutes or less of prep time. You just toss the ingredients in your slow cooker in the morning and come home to a tasty, nutritious meal.

Using a slow cooker enables you to build flavor into the foods you cook without putting in much time or fuss. In many cases, recipes can be doubled to save even more time, since you cook once and eat twice—a great time-saver for people who don't want to spend a lot of time in the kitchen but still want to benefit from healthy DASH-diet home cooking. Many of the recipes also freeze well, so you can prepare them ahead of time and pull them out of the freezer for a quick meal on the go.

If you're trying to make a healthy diet change and you want easy and delicious recipes, this is the cookbook for you. It will minimize the time you spend in the kitchen while maximizing the healthfulness of the foods you eat—and perk up your menus at the same time. Whether you're a vegan or a carnivore, whether your tastes run to the exotic or the familiar, you'll find tasty dishes here that are easy to cook. Get ready to enjoy the pleasures of eating well!

DASH Diet 101

Before jumping into information about how you can use your slow cooker to create delicious DASH diet–friendly meals, it may be helpful to review the basics of the DASH diet. If you're already familiar with the diet and its principles, then feel free to skip ahead to chapter 2.

If you're following the DASH diet, you've already made the decision to take better care of your heart health. Congratulations on making a healthy choice for your overall well-being! Studies of the DASH diet, including one in the July 2001 issue of the *American Journal of Clinical Nutrition*, show that eating this way is likely to reduce the risk factors of coronary artery disease. Combining the diet with exercise and weight loss provides even more protection, according to the ENCORE study, as published in the January 25, 2010, issue of *JAMA Internal Medicine*. Studies like these show that the DASH diet is a heart-healthy way to eat.

DASH Diet Basics

The DASH (Dietary Approaches to Stop Hypertension) diet provides a template for heart-healthy eating, particularly for people who are seeking a dietary approach to lower high blood pressure (hypertension) and improve blood lipids (cholesterol). While it isn't technically a weight-loss diet, combining it with a reduction in calories can help you achieve your weight-loss goals.

The diet is quite flexible and can be customized to your own personal tastes and needs. You can adjust calorie levels to your body size, activity level, and weight goals, and you can pick and choose from a variety of food groups. Unlike other diets, the DASH diet doesn't omit or limit any macronutrients (protein, fat, carbs) or food groups (fruits, vegetables, grains/starches, meat/fish/protein, dairy, fats, legumes/nuts/seeds), but rather helps you make healthy, balanced choices from among all the food groups.

TWO TYPES OF DASH DIET

According to the Mayo Clinic, there are two types of DASH diet: the standard DASH diet and the lower-sodium DASH diet. On the standard DASH diet, you can consume up to 2,300 milligrams of sodium daily. On the lower-sodium DASH diet, you are allowed up to 1,500 milligrams of sodium daily. Both versions of the diet can help reduce blood pressure, but certain populations may benefit from the lower-sodium version of the diet. You should consider the lower-sodium DASH diet if you:

- » Are over 51 years of age
- » Are African-American
- » Have high blood pressure (hypertension)
- » Have diabetes
- » Have chronic kidney disease

FOOD GROUP RECOMMENDATIONS

Along with recommendations for lower sodium intake, the DASH diet also recommends eating the following every day:

- » 6 to 8 servings of whole grains
- » 4 to 5 servings of vegetables
- » 4 to 5 servings of fruits
- » 2 to 3 servings of low-fat dairy
- » 6 or fewer servings of lean meat, poultry, and fish
- » 2 to 3 servings of healthy fats and oils

The plan also has some weekly recommendations:

- » 4 to 5 servings per week of nuts, seeds, and legumes
- » 5 or fewer servings per week of sweets

Other aspects of the plan include limiting how much alcohol and caffeine you drink, which can increase blood pressure.

A single serving of rice is not the same size as a single serving of potatoes, although they are both in the same food group, so refer to the chart on page 12 and the recipes themselves for information on how many servings of each food group are in each recipe in this book. Each recipe lists the servings per food group for one serving of that dish. For example, if the dish serves four people, the food group servings assume that each person is eating one-quarter of the whole dish.

Foods to Enjoy and Foods to Avoid

Whole Grains and Starches

ENJOY Brown rice • Oatmeal • Whole-wheat flour • Whole-wheat pasta • Barley • Quinoa • Wild rice • Corn • Sweet potatoes • Whole grain crackers

AVOID White rice • Instant oatmeal • White flour • White pasta • Chips • Processed crunchy snacks

Vegetables

ENJOY Leafy greens (spinach, kale, mustard greens, lettuce) • Cruciferous vegetables (broccoli, cabbage, cauliflower, etc.) • Root vegetables (onions, carrots, turnips, beets, potatoes, etc.) • Peppers (bell peppers, chile peppers) • Artichokes • Asparagus • Radishes • Mushrooms • Celery • Fennel • Green beans • Tomatoes

AVOID Vegetables canned with salt and preservatives • Fried potatoes (French fries, chips) • Canned tomato or pasta sauce, if high in sodium

Fruits

ENJOY Stone fruits (peaches, plums, apricots, cherries, etc.) • Tree fruits (apples, pears, etc.) • Citrus fruits (oranges, lemons, limes, grapefruit, etc.) • Grapes • Berries (blueberries, strawberries, raspberries, etc.) • Tropical fruits (bananas, mangos, pineapple, papaya, etc.) • Avocados

AVOID Fruit canned in syrup

Meat, Poultry, and Fish

ENJOY Lean ground beef • Lean beef cuts • Skinless poultry (turkey, chicken, etc.) • Ground turkey breast • Ground chicken breast • Low-sodium turkey bacon • Low-sodium Canadian bacon • Low-sodium ham • Lean pork (tenderloin, cuts trimmed of excess fat) • Fish and shellfish (cod, halibut, shrimp, clams, salmon, etc.) • Tofu • Seitan • Egg whites

AVOID Fatty beef cuts • High-fat ground beef • Skin-on poultry • Processed meats (pepperoni, sausage, etc.) • Hot dogs • Bacon • Deli meats (unless low sodium) • Fried chicken • Fried fish sticks • Fish and chips

Dairy

ENJOY Skim milk • Fat-free or low-fat yogurt (plain) • Fat-free or low-fat sour cream • Fat-free or low-fat cheese

AVOID Heavy cream • Whole milk • Butter • Full-fat cheese • Full-fat yogurt • Ice cream • Half-and-half

Fats and Oils

ENJOY Extra-virgin olive oil • Canola oil • Margarine • Low-fat or fat-free mayonnaise • Low-fat or fat-free salad dressing

AVOID Butter • Lard • Shortening

Nuts, Seeds, and Legumes

ENJOY Dried beans • Canned beans (low sodium) • Nuts (unsalted) • Seeds (unsalted) • Canned peas (low sodium) • Fresh peas • Frozen peas

AVOID Salted nuts • Salted seeds • Canned beans (high sodium) • Canned peas (high sodium)

Beverages

ENJOY Water • Unsweetened fruit or vegetable juice • Coffee (decaf) • Tea (decaf) • Soda (diet, in moderation, and not replacing water)

AVOID Coffee (caffeinated) • Tea (caffeinated) • Alcohol • Juice (sweetened) • Soda (not diet) • Sweetened beverages such as Kool-Aid • Energy drinks

Herbs, Spices, and Condiments

ENJOY Dried herbs • Fresh herbs • Dried spices • Pepper • Low-fat or fat-free mayonnaise • Mustard • Low-sugar ketchup • Low-fat salad dressings • Vinegar

AVOID Ketchup (regular) • Full-fat salad dressing

General DASH Guidelines

Food Group	Daily Servings (1,200-calorie diet)	Daily Servings (2,000-calorie diet)	Serving Size	Examples
WHOLE GRAINS & STARCHES	5	7 to 8	• 1 ounce dry	• ½ cup cooked whole-wheat pasta • ½ cup cooked brown rice • ½ cup cooked oatmeal • 1 slice whole-wheat bread
ANIMAL PROTEIN (Lean Meat, Poultry, Fish & Eggs)	4 or fewer	6 or fewer	• 1 ounce fish, meat, poultry • 2 egg whites • 1 whole egg	• 1 ounce cooked turkey breast • Omelet made from 2 egg whites • 1 scrambled egg
VEGETABLES	3	5	• 1 cup raw leafy greens • ½ cup cooked or raw cut vegetables • 4 ounces vegetable juice	• 1 cup spinach • ½ cup cooked spinach • ½ cup raw carrot sticks • 4 ounces tomato juice (low-sodium)
FRUITS	3	5	• ½ cup berries or cut fruit • 1 medium fruit • ¼ cup dried fruit • 4 ounces unsweetened fruit juice	• ½ cup blueberries • ½ cup unsweetened pineapple chunks • 1 medium apple • 1 medium orange • 1 medium banana • ¼ cup raisins • ¼ cup dried apples • 4 ounces apple juice • 4 ounces lemon or lime juice

The icons in this chart appear with every recipe to indicate servings by food group.

General DASH Guidelines

Food Group	Daily Servings (1,200-calorie diet)	Daily Servings (2,000-calorie diet)	Serving Size	Examples
DAIRY	2	3	• 8 ounces low-fat milk • 1 cup fat-free yogurt, sour cream, cottage cheese • ½ ounce low-fat cheese	• 1 cup skim milk • 1 cup plain fat-free yogurt • ½ ounce grated low-fat Cheddar cheese
FATS & OILS	2	3	• 1 teaspoon vegetable oil • 1 teaspoon margarine • 1 tablespoon low-fat mayonnaise • 2 tablespoons reduced-fat salad dressing	• 1 teaspoon extra-virgin olive oil • 1 teaspoon soft margarine • 2 tablespoons low-fat Italian vinaigrette
NUTS, SEEDS & LEGUMES	3 per week	5 per week	• 2 tablespoons nut butter • ⅓ cup unsalted nuts • 2 tablespoons seeds • ½ cup cooked legumes	• 2 tablespoons unsalted almond butter • ⅓ cup unsalted cashews • 2 tablespoons chia seeds • ½ cup cooked lentils
SWEETS	3 per week or fewer	5 per week or fewer	• 1 tablespoon sugar • 2 hard candies • 1 tablespoon jam • 8 ounces sweetened beverage	• 1 tablespoon white sugar • 2 peppermint candies • 1 tablespoon grape jelly • 8 ounces sweetened juice
SODIUM LIMIT	1,500 mg to 2,300 mg	1,500 mg to 2,300 mg	• ½ to 1 teaspoon added salt	—

EAT WHOLE FOODS

The standard Western diet is filled with processed foods, foods high in sugar, and lots of empty calories. While eating these foods is convenient, it isn't the best thing for your health. Processed and fast foods tend to be high in sodium, fat, protein, and an array of chemical ingredients that don't nourish the body.

For your best health, it's important to eat foods that are nutrient dense—that is, foods that contain a high level of nutrition per calorie. Processed foods typically don't meet this standard, but whole foods do. Whole foods are those that are as close to their natural state as possible, and include fresh fruits and vegetables; whole, unprocessed grains; lean meats, poultry, and seafood; low-fat dairy; nuts, seeds, and legumes; minimally processed oils; and fresh or dried herbs and spices. Using these foods as the basic ingredients for your cooking will provide nutrition while minimizing artificial chemicals, salt, sugar, and empty calories.

Daily Calorie Intake

While not technically a weight-loss program, watching your calorie intake on the DASH diet is an essential part of healthy eating. Calories are a measure of the energy that food provides your body when you eat it. Keeping track of how many calories you eat, versus how many you need, is important when you are trying to gain, lose, or maintain weight. When you eat more calories than your body burns, the net result is typically weight gain. When you eat fewer calories than your body requires, the net result is weight loss. Therefore, it's important to know your own caloric requirements.

The amount of calories your body needs to maintain your weight depends on a number of factors, including:

» Age	» Height
» Gender	» Activity level
» Weight	

Many people tend to overestimate the number or calories they need to maintain their current weight, and they also often overestimate how many calories they burn through activity.

To lose weight, you need to eat fewer calories than you burn. You can do this through a combination of reducing the number of calories you eat and increasing your activity level. For example, a woman of average height who is slightly overweight with a low to moderate activity level needs 1,700 to 1,800 calories per day to maintain her weight. To lose weight, she'll need to eat 400 to 500 fewer calories a day to lose about one pound a week (a pound equals about 3,200 calories; remember, that's spread out over seven days). This means she'll need to eat about 1,200 calories a day to lose weight.

To determine your calorie requirements, use a calorie calculator. You can find great resources online, such as Active.com's calorie calculator: www.active.com/fitness/calculators /calories. Then determine the number of calories you'll need to lose about a pound per week. Many fitness and nutrition experts recommend eating no fewer than 1,200 calories a day to maintain good health, and caution against long-term extreme calorie restriction below this point, because it can trigger hunger, cravings, and loss of energy.

Weekly Meal Tracker

Use the following tracker for your meals. First, put the number of servings you require (daily or weekly) in the left column. Then, make a tally mark on the appropriate day every time you have one serving of that food group. When you've reached your max for the day or week, circle your marks in that box so you'll know you're done with that group.

	Mon	Tue	Wed	Thu	Fri	Sat	Sun
WHOLE GRAINS & STARCHES ———— Servings per day							
ANIMAL PROTEIN ———— Servings per day							
VEGETABLES ———— Servings per day							
FRUITS ———— Servings per day							
DAIRY ———— Servings per day							
FATS & OILS ———— Servings per day							
NUTS, SEEDS & LEGUMES ———— Servings per day							
SWEETS ———— Servings per day							

2

DASH into Slow Cooking

It's easy to get caught up in the idea that a slow cooker won't work for the DASH diet. After all, the DASH diet maximizes vegetables and minimizes fatty meats, which are traditionally thought of as best for the slow cooker. However, using the right amounts of liquid and seasonings, you can make DASH-friendly meals just as delicious as anything that comes out of your slow cooker. In fact, you will likely find that using your slow cooker helps make it easier to follow the DASH diet, because it saves time spent in the kitchen.

In this chapter you'll find the information you need to not only make the tasty recipes in this cookbook, but also to start to create your own DASH diet–friendly meals. Your slow cooker will become your go-to for making healthy, quick, flavorful, DASH-compatible foods.

Slow Cooking the DASH Way

If you're still not convinced that a slow cooker is a fantastic and flavorful choice for cooking your DASH meals, consider this:

» **You'll spend less active time prepping and cooking.** In most of the recipes in this book, the most labor-intensive thing you'll do is chop vegetables, and in many cases you can substitute precut or frozen vegetables for fresh ones, so you don't even have to chop. After 15 minutes or less of prep, you can set the timer on your slow cooker and walk away.

» **It's the perfect cooking method for people with busy lives.** Sometimes when you spend a long day at work or running kids around, you're too exhausted to cook when you get home. Using a slow cooker means you don't have to cook after a long, tiring day. Instead, you come home to a hot meal that's ready to go.

» **It can help you stay on track with your eating plan.** Have you ever, after that long, tiring day, decided not to cook and instead to grab some takeout? Many people do this. Having a healthy meal ready in your slow cooker when you get home can keep you on track and prevent you from heading for high-fat, high-salt fast food.

» **It's perfect for cooking ahead.** Another way to stay on track with any diet is to cook meals ahead of time and refrigerate or freeze them for the week to come. A slow cooker allows you to do this with minimal hands-on time. You can double or triple recipes in many cases, so you can freeze meals for quick dining on the go.

» **Slow cooking intensifies flavor.** Many people worry that the DASH diet is flavorless because it is low in salt, but cooking in a slow cooker over several hours lets flavors build and intensify.

Slow Cooker Basics

The slow cooker is one of the easiest kitchen appliances to use. There's not much more to it than filling it up and turning it on. That said, having some basic knowledge can help ensure the success of your meals.

SIZE AND SHAPE

Slow cookers range in size from super tiny one- or two-person cookers to extra-large 6- or 7-quart behemoths. You can also find slow cookers with round or oval crocks. The recipes in this cookbook are written for a slow cooker that has a 5- to 7.5-quart oval crock. Slow cookers in this size and shape can best fit different cuts of meat, and they make sure you have plenty of room for a single recipe or, in many cases, to double it or triple it. This is the ideal size slow cooker for an average size family, and most recipes you'll find are written for slow cookers of this size. If your slow cooker is a different size, you may need to double or halve recipes. For slow cookers of different shapes, you may need to trim roasts and vegetables for a better fit.

CONTROLS

You will find slow cookers with manual controls (usually a dial) or programmable electronic controls. Both work well. Models with dial controls tend to be a little less expensive. However, electronic controls enable you to program the slow cooker to cook on high or low for a certain time, then switch to a keep warm setting. This is ideal for people who want to cook dinner while they're at work all day and then allow the food to remain warm until they get home. Choose the type that works best for your needs and budget.

COOKING TEMPERATURE AND TIME

Your slow cooker is very different from your stove top. On your stove, you can control the temperature from very high to very low. In fact, you can use your stove for braising, just as you do in the slow cooker, although cooking times are much shorter (usually one to three hours on low heat on the stove). And you'll need to babysit anything on the stove, regardless of the temperature.

This isn't the case with your slow cooker. In most slow cookers, you have three heat settings: low, high, and keep warm. In general, when you're starting with raw (not frozen) meat, you'll use the following cooking times:

» Low: 7 to 9 hours
» High: 3 to 6 hours

In other words, low takes about twice as long as high. It's important to note, however, that cooking time may vary by as much as 2 hours, depending on the temperature of your slow cooker. There's not a lot of consistency between brands or models, so you may want to take some time to get to know your own slow cooker's quirks. For that reason, it may be best to plan to be home all day the first time you use your slow cooker, so you can monitor how quickly it cooks.

OVERCOOKING

When you overcook food in your slow cooker, it can get dried out, stringy, and not very palatable. Fortunately, it's relatively difficult to overcook foods once you know your slow cooker's limitations. To avoid overcooking:

» Get to know your slow cooker and adjust cooking time accordingly. Once meat cooks, switch the slow cooker over to keep low (a programmable thermometer is perfect for this).
» Cook meats whole or in large cuts instead of cutting them into small pieces, which will keep meat from overcooking.
» Use plenty of moisture in the pot, particularly with lean meats.
» Don't open the slow cooker lid while your dish is cooking.
» For long cooking times, braise on low and then, as soon as the meat is cooked, shift it to keep warm until you're ready to eat. If you're normally away from home when this happens, you'll probably want to consider a programmable timer.
» Use the right size slow cooker for the job. For example, if you find your food is overcooking, you may wish to double a recipe so the food will cook more slowly.

BEST FOODS FOR SLOW COOKING

Some foods work better in the slow cooker than others.

» Fatty, tough cuts of meat tend to work better than extra-lean cuts. You don't need to leave the big chunks of fat on the outside of the meat, however. Instead, trim those away and leave the intramuscular fat in place. Then, defat the dish before serving (see the box below).

» Dark meat poultry works better than white meat poultry in the slow cooker.

» Fish and seafood work best when added later in the cooking process.

» Vegetables and fruits can be stewed all day, as can broths. You can use either fresh fruits and vegetables or precut frozen. They work equally well.

» Grains and legumes work well as long as you leave the lid on and use the proper amount of liquid.

» There's no need to use fresh herbs, because the slow cooker will cook them down anyway. Instead, save time and money and cook with dried herbs and spices.

TO PREP OR NOT TO PREP

When working with a slow cooker, there are two types of prep:

» Essential prep includes peeling and chopping everything so it's ready for your dish.

» Nonessential prep includes browning meats or vegetables to add more flavor to your dish.

Using Your Slow Cooker: Do's and Don'ts

» **DO** make sure your slow cooker is at least half full. If it isn't, double the recipe.

» **DO** add liquid to lean meats to keep them moist while cooking.

» **DO** defat any liquid in the slow cooker before serving by using a spoon to skim excess fat from the top.

» **DO** submerge any meat in liquid to keep it moist while cooking.

» **DON'T** fill the slow cooker more than two-thirds full, because you may wind up with undercooked food.

» **DON'T** start with frozen meat in the slow cooking process, or it's likely the meat won't get fully cooked.

» **DON'T** lift the lid while slow cooking—you need the moisture and heat to stay inside and keep everything tender and fully cooked.

» **DON'T** add dairy until the end of cooking, or it could curdle.

The recipes in this book don't require nonessential prep—although they do offer tips for doing so. Starting with raw ingredients is just fine, and your dishes will be packed with flavor. However, you can kick it up one more notch by browning meats and vegetables on the stove top first, to add a deeper flavor to your dishes. If you have a bit more time, consider trying the following nonessential prep steps:

» Sauté meats and vegetables in a hot pan with a tablespoon or two of olive oil. Sauté whole pieces of poultry or meat for 3 to 5 minutes per side, and then use a little liquid to deglaze the pan before adding everything to the slow cooker. You can also sauté chopped aromatic vegetables, such as onions, carrots, and celery, in a little olive oil in a nonstick sauté pan on medium high for 3 to 5 minutes.

» Roasting meats, bones, and aromatic vegetables such as carrots, fennel, and onions can help bring out the flavors before adding them to the slow cooker. Toss the ingredients with a little oil and brown them in a 450˚F oven for about 20 minutes.

» Browning isn't essential for ground meats or chopped vegetables, but it can help with texture while cooking. Brown ground beef, ground pork, ground poultry, and chopped carrots, celery, or onions in a little olive oil on medium-high, stirring as you cook, until browned, about 5 minutes.

FOOD SAFETY

Nobody wants to be sick with food poisoning, so it's important you cook foods to a particular temperature and also maintain them at a certain temperature to keep them safe. Here are some tips for safe food handling:

» Always thaw meat. Don't add frozen meat to your slow cooker because it can drop the temperature to unsafe levels, or may not cook in the allotted time.

» Cook only on low or high. Do not cook on keep warm.

» Hold foods on keep warm for a maximum of 2 hours.

» Reheat leftovers on the stove or in the microwave, not in a slow cooker.

» Always soak dried legumes for at least 12 hours, and rinse them before putting them in a slow cooker.

» Use a food thermometer to check the temperature before serving. Bacteria can grow in undercooked foods. Beef and lamb should be at least 145°F to 150°F. Pork, poultry, sauces, soups, and stews need to be at least 165°F.

» Refrigerate leftovers right away in a clean container. Don't refrigerate them in the crock of the slow cooker, and don't allow them to cool on the countertop.

» Put the vegetables in the slow cooker before any meat, so they are on the bottom.

» Keep food refrigerated until you're ready to add them to the slow cooker, as bacteria can grow quickly at room temperature.

Socket Timers

If you don't have a programmable slow cooker, you can still set your slow cooker to cook at a time that is more convenient to your schedule by using a socket timer. A socket timer is a simple plug-in accessory that you set to turn on power to your slow cooker whenever you want. Most hardware stores sell them; many people use them to turn their lights on and off when they are on vacation.

With a socket timer, you can set your slow cooker for the right cooking time, which means you can be away from the house for more than 8 hours without fear of overcooking your food and arriving home to a dry (or mushy), unpalatable meal. This is a great way to customize cooking times if you have a nonprogrammable slow cooker, since you don't want to overcook foods if you're going to be away.

To use a socket timer:

1. Plug the timer into your outlet.
2. Plug the slow cooker into the timer.
3. Set the timer for the time you would like it to start cooking (plan 8 hours from the time the cooker starts to mealtime).
4. Turn the slow cooker to low (don't worry; it won't turn on until the time you set).

When using a socket timer, be sure all the ingredients you put in your slow cooker are very cold (but not frozen). This will help them remain cold until the timer turns on. Don't set your timer for more than 2 hours later, because you don't want your food growing bacteria while it waits.

Freezing and Storing

Your slow cooker is the ideal vessel for making freezable meals. In most cases, slow cooker meals freeze really well with minimal loss of flavor or texture. The following foods freeze extremely well:

» Soups and stews

» Cooked meats

» Cooked rice or other grains

» Cooked legumes

These foods don't freeze as well from a flavor and/or texture standpoint, although safety-wise, they are fine:

» Eggs

» Dairy

» Pasta

Consider the following storage tips:

» Freeze in single-serving containers.

» Thaw in your refrigerator overnight or in the microwave on the thaw setting.

» Freeze for up to 1 year.

» Always date and label leftovers so you know what's in the container and when you need to discard it.

» Never refreeze reheated meals. Discard them.

» Freeze in tightly sealed containers such as plastic containers with tight-sealing lids or resealable freezer bags.

» Don't fill the storage container completely. Allow a little room for expansion as the food freezes.

» Don't put hot foods in the freezer. Cool them first in the refrigerator and then transfer to the freezer.

Tips and Tricks for Delicious Slow-Cooked DASH Meals

While health is important, making your DASH meals tasty is also essential, because flavorful food makes it easier to follow a special diet. Consider the following tips for making your meals delicious:

» **Add herbs and spices.** Herbs and spices are super flavorful, and they add a lot to your slow cooker meals. When slow cooking, dried herbs lend a more potent flavor than fresh, since the slow cooker obliterates fresh herbs' very freshness. If you do want to use fresh herbs, stir them in at the very end of cooking.

» **Add a little salt.** While the DASH diet is a low-sodium diet, adding a little salt helps bring out the flavors of foods. Using ½ teaspoon salt (recommended in most of the recipes) spread out over four to six servings makes a big flavor difference, and it doesn't add a lot of sodium. You aren't adding salt to make things taste "salty," but rather to enhance the other flavors in your dish. Sea salt tastes just a bit "saltier" than table salt, so you get the most bang for your buck with this ingredient.

» **Trim the fat.** You're going to want to defat twice with your slow cooker when you're using fatty cuts of meat. First, cut away fat from the outside of the meat, but leave the intramuscular fat, which will help retain moisture while cooking. Then, use a spoon to skim as much of the fat as possible from the sauce after cooking, and discard any large chunks of fat that may remain.

» **Add texture.** If you want vegetables with a little crunch, add them later in the cooking. Adding them at the beginning of cooking is fine, but if you're looking for a texture contrast, add them in the last few hours for a bit more bite.

» **Thicken sauces by simmering.** If you want a thicker sauce, you'll need to simmer it on the stove after you're done cooking in the slow cooker. Simmer it in a shallow, uncovered pan over medium heat until it reaches your desired texture.

» **Thicken sauces by puréeing the vegetables.** You can also thicken soups or sauces by spooning out the vegetables, particularly carrots, and puréeing them in a blender or food processor before stirring them back into the slow cooker.

» **Make your vegetable pieces the same size.** This way, the vegetables will need the same cook time and have the same texture.

» **Stir in cooked pasta, rice, or other grains at the end.** Otherwise, you'll wind up with mushy grains, and nobody wants that!

» **Get to know your own slow cooker.** Cooking times are approximate, because every slow cooker's temperature and cooking speed vary. Spend some time testing your slow cooker, and adjust your cooking times accordingly.

About the Recipes in This Book

You're just about ready to get started with your delicious slow cooker DASH cooking. The recipes in the following chapters were specially developed to help you cook DASH diet–friendly foods with minimal prep time.

The recipes are designed for a 5- to 7.5-quart slow cooker. They all include fewer than ten ingredients (not counting salt and pepper), and prep times are minimal—15 minutes or less—making it easy for you to incorporate healthy DASH foods into your busy life. With just 15 minutes or less of prep in the morning, you can come home in 8 hours to a fully cooked, healthy meal.

A few recipes cook for less than 8 hours, which is great for weekends and days off. For recipes with shorter cooking times, or for days when you are away for longer, consider using a socket timer (see the sidebar on page 22). Alternatively, you can set your slow cooker's program feature to adjust to keep warm after the requisite cooking time.

You'll also notice that the recipes have tips for prep if you have time to do more, suggestions for making a balanced meal, and shopping tips. These will help you more effectively manage your time as you cook. Also, some of the recipes are labeled "super quick prep," indicating recipes that can be prepped in less than 10 minutes.

Cooking for Two?

While the recipes in this book serve four to six, all are adjustable both upward and downward. If you are cooking for two:

» Halve all the ingredients in the recipe. You may need to add a bit more liquid to ensure all meat is submerged as you cook.

» Consider investing in a smaller slow cooker. A 1.5-quart slow cooker is ideal for this purpose.

» The cooking time remains the same, provided you're using a smaller slow cooker and fewer ingredients.

» You can also cook the entire recipe and dine on leftovers, or freeze them for a quick meal later (see freezing tips on page 22). This will save you time throughout the week as you go about your busy schedule.

Kitchen Staples

Vegetable Broth

MAKES ABOUT 10 CUPS • **PREP TIME:** 5 MINUTES • **COOK TIME:** 8 TO 12 HOURS
Super Quick Prep

This is a great way to use up vegetable trimmings. When you use vegetables in other dishes, fill a resealable bag with the clean trimmings and skins from onions, celery, carrots, fennel, mushrooms, garlic, and fresh herbs. Keep the bag of trimmings in the freezer, and when you're ready to make stock, just dump a gallon-size bag of trimmings into the slow cooker and cover it with water. Alternatively, you can use the ingredients below.

4 ounces fresh mushrooms

2 celery stalks (leaves included), roughly chopped

2 carrots, roughly chopped

1 onion, roughly chopped

1 head garlic, halved crosswise

2 fresh thyme sprigs

10 peppercorns

1. In your slow cooker, combine all the ingredients. Add water to fill the slow cooker two-thirds of the way.

2. Cover and set on low. Cook for 8 to 12 hours.

3. Strain the broth through a fine-mesh sieve, discarding the solids.

4. Store the broth in an airtight container in the refrigerator for up to 5 days or in the freezer for up to 1 year.

PRECOOKING TIP If you want to get more flavor from the vegetables in the stock, roast them in a 450˚F oven for about 30 minutes before adding them to the slow cooker.

PER SERVING (1 Cup) Calories: 35; Total Fat: 0g; Saturated Fat: 0g; Cholesterol: 0mg; Carbohydrates: 4g; Fiber: 0g; Protein: 0g; Sodium:13mg; Potassium: 114mg

Poultry Broth

MAKES ABOUT 10 CUPS • **PREP TIME:** 5 MINUTES • **COOK TIME:** 12 TO 24 HOURS
Super Quick Prep

The longer you cook this poultry broth, the more flavorful it will be, with benefits maxing out at about 24 hours, after which the broth may grow bitter. This is a great use for poultry parts typically thrown away, such as wings, necks, backs, gizzards, or even feet. Don't use the liver, which will add bitter flavors. You can also use a picked-over carcass from a cooked chicken, turkey, or duck. Leaving the broth unsalted gives you total control over salt levels when you cook with it later on.

1 chicken or turkey carcass or 1 pound raw chicken or turkey pieces

2 carrots, roughly chopped

1 onion, quartered

2 celery stalks, roughly chopped

1 head garlic, halved crosswise

2 fresh rosemary sprigs

10 peppercorns

1. In your slow cooker, combine all the ingredients. Add water to fill the slow cooker two-thirds of the way.

2. Cover and set on low. Cook for 12 to 24 hours.

3. Strain the broth through a fine-mesh sieve, discarding the solids.

4. Cover the broth and refrigerate it for 2 to 3 hours.

5. Use a spoon to skim the fat from the top of the stock and discard it.

6. Store the broth in an airtight container in the refrigerator for up to 5 days or in the freezer for up to 1 year.

SMART SHOPPING TIP Save money by keeping a bag of leftover poultry bones and fresh vegetable trimmings in the freezer. Then, use the contents of the bag to make your stock.

PER SERVING (1 Cup) Calories: 73; Total Fat: 3g; Saturated Fat: 1g; Cholesterol: 7mg; Carbohydrates: 8g; Fiber: 0g; Protein: 6g; Sodium: 97mg; Potassium: 254mg

Beef Broth

MAKES ABOUT 10 CUPS • **PREP TIME:** 5 MINUTES • **COOK TIME:** 24 TO 48 HOURS
Super Quick Prep

Meat broth works well in recipes that require richer, heartier flavors. The trick to making a good meat broth is using the bones. This flavors the broth and, with 24 to 48 hours of simmering, also pulls many of the minerals from the bones into the broth to make it rich and nourishing. Check whether your butcher has bones available to make this versatile and tasty broth. The longer you simmer the broth, the more flavorful it becomes; however, don't simmer for longer than 48 hours or it may turn bitter.

2 to 3 pounds beef bones and trimmings

4 ounces fresh mushrooms or 1 ounce dried mushrooms

1 carrot, roughly chopped

1 celery stalk (leaves included), roughly chopped

1 onion, roughly chopped

1 head garlic, halved crosswise

1 fresh rosemary sprig

1 fresh thyme sprig

14 peppercorns

1. In your slow cooker, combine all the ingredients. Add water to fill the slow cooker two-thirds of the way.

2. Cover and set on low. Cook for 24 to 48 hours.

3. Strain the broth through a fine-mesh sieve, discarding the solids.

4. Cover the broth and refrigerate it for 2 to 3 hours.

5. Use a spoon to skim the fat from the top of the stock and discard it.

6. Store the broth in an airtight container in the refrigerator for up to 5 days or in the freezer for up to 1 year.

PER SERVING (1 Cup) Calories: 56; Total Fat: 0g; Saturated Fat: 0g; Cholesterol: 0mg; Carbohydrates: 3g; Fiber: 0g; Protein: 5g; Sodium: 62mg; Potassium: 198mg

Brown Rice

MAKES ABOUT 6 CUPS • **PREP TIME:** 5 MINUTES • **COOK TIME:** 2 TO 4 HOURS
Super Quick Prep

Precooking rice in your slow cooker is a great weekend project. It takes only a few hours to get 6 cups of rice, which you can then store in ½-cup portions in resealable bags in the refrigerator to use in recipes throughout the week. Or, put the bags in the freezer and then thaw the rice in the refrigerator overnight or in the microwave for 1 minute. You can even add frozen rice to the dish in your slow cooker about 2 hours before serving and let it thaw as your food finishes cooking. Feel free to double the recipe if needed, so you have plenty of cooked rice. While this recipe suggests cooking the rice in stock, you can also cook it in water for a more neutral flavor.

Nonstick cooking spray

2 cups brown rice

3⅓ cups Vegetable Broth (page 28), Poultry Broth (page 29), Beef Broth (page 30), or store bought

1 tablespoon olive oil

1. Spray the crock of your slow cooker with nonstick cooking spray.
2. Add the rice, broth, and olive oil, stirring to combine.
3. Cover and set on high. Cook, stirring every hour or so, until the rice is fluffy, 2 to 4 hours.

SMART SHOPPING TIP Buy rice in bulk at the grocery store to save money.

PER SERVING (½ Cup) Calories: 126; Total Fat: 2g; Saturated Fat: 0g; Cholesterol: 0mg; Carbohydrates: 24g; Fiber: 1g; Protein: 3g; Sodium: 14mg; Potassium: 201mg

Quinoa

MAKES 6 CUPS • **PREP TIME:** 5 MINUTES • **COOK TIME:** 6 HOURS
Super Quick Prep

Making quinoa in the slow cooker is another excellent cook-ahead weekend project. Refrigerate or freeze the cooked quinoa in ½-cup portions in resealable bags for quick reheating throughout the week. Thaw frozen quinoa in your refrigerator overnight, or put it in the microwave for 1 minute. You can also add the frozen quinoa to your meal in the slow cooker about 2 hours before serving and let the food in the slow cooker warm it up. This recipe works equally well with any type of quinoa.

Nonstick cooking spray

2 cups quinoa

4 cups Vegetable Broth (page 28), Poultry Broth (page 29), Beef Broth (page 30), or store bought

1 tablespoon olive oil

1. Spray the crock of your slow cooker with nonstick cooking spray.
2. Add the quinoa, broth, and olive oil, stirring to combine.
3. Cover and set on low. Cook for about 6 hours. Fluff with a fork.

PRECOOKING TIP Rinsing the quinoa before you cook it helps wash away any bitter flavors. Put the quinoa in a fine-mesh sieve, and rinse it for about 30 seconds under cold running water.

PER SERVING (½ Cup) Calories: 106; Total Fat: 2g; Saturated Fat: 0g; Cholesterol: 0mg; Carbohydrates: 18g; Fiber: 2g; Protein: 4g; Sodium: 9mg; Potassium: 210mg

Lentils

MAKES 6 CUPS • **PREP TIME:** 5 MINUTES • **COOK TIME:** 7 TO 8 HOURS
Super Quick Prep

Having cooked lentils on hand means you can quickly add them to soups and stews. They also make a delicious side dish when cooked with aromatic vegetables and herbs. While this is a bare-bones lentil recipe, feel free to add chopped carrot, onion, celery, garlic, and/or thyme to the slow cooker for more flavorful lentils. This recipe works with all types of dried lentils. Refrigerate or freeze the cooked lentils in ½-cup portions in resealable bags for use throughout the week.

3 cups dried lentils, soaked
   overnight and rinsed

6 cups Vegetable Broth
   (page 28), Poultry Broth
   (page 29), Beef Broth
   (page 30), or store bought

1. In your slow cooker, combine the lentils and broth.
2. Cover and set on low. Cook until the lentils are soft, 7 to 8 hours.

PER SERVING (½ Cup) Calories: 172; Total Fat: 1g; Saturated Fat: 0g; Cholesterol: 0mg; Carbohydrates: 29g; Fiber: 15g; Protein: 13g; Sodium: 17mg; Potassium: 572mg

PRECOOKING TIP Pick over the lentils before using them, in order to remove any small stones or bits of plant debris. Then, rinse them in a colander under running water for about 30 seconds.

Beans

MAKES 6 CUPS • **PREP TIME:** 5 MINUTES • **COOK TIME:** 6 TO 8 HOURS
Super Quick Prep

This basic recipe works with any type of dried beans, such as white beans, black beans, and kidney beans. Store ½-cup portions of the cooked beans in resealable bags so you'll have some on hand whenever you need them. Cooking beans in water (or, if you like, in salt-free vegetable, poultry, or beef broth) is a great way to minimize sodium, since most canned beans contain added salt.

1 pound dried beans, soaked
   overnight and rinsed

1 bay leaf

1. In your slow cooker, combine the beans and bay leaf.
2. Add enough water to come just about ½ inch over the top of the beans.
3. Cover and cook on low until the beans are soft, 6 to 8 hours.

PRECOOKING TIP Soaking your beans in water overnight makes them a lot less gassy.

PER SERVING (½ Cup) Calories: 127; Total Fat: 1g; Saturated Fat: 0g; Cholesterol: 0mg; Carbohydrates: 23g; Fiber: 9g; Protein: 8g; Sodium: 2mg; Potassium: 79mg

Pearl Barley

MAKES 4 CUPS • **PREP TIME:** 10 MINUTES • **COOK TIME:** 8 HOURS
Super Quick Prep

Cooked barley is great to have around. Store this in one-cup servings in your freezer, and you'll always have some barley to toss into soups or stews, or to serve as a side dish mixed with veggies, herbs, and spices. It's a tasty alternative to rice, couscous, potatoes, and other starchy sides.

2 cups pearl barley   ½ teaspoon salt
5 cups boiling water

1. Combine all ingredients in your slow cooker.
2. Cover and cook on low for 8 hours.

PER SERVING (½ Cup) Calories: 352; Total Fat: 1.2g; Saturated Fat: 0g; Cholesterol: 0mg; Carbohydrates: 78g; Fiber 16g; Protein: 10g; Sodium: 309mg; Potassium: 283mg

Soups

Golden Mushroom Soup

SERVES 6 • **PREP TIME:** 10 MINUTES • **COOK TIME:** 8 HOURS

Super Quick Prep

This delicious mushroom soup is easy to throw together in the morning before you leave the house. It makes a tasty lunch or dinner, and it's easy to keep it vegan or vegetarian by choosing the type of stock you use. Make it heartier for dinner by adding some cooked brown rice or quinoa to the soup just before you serve it.

1 onion, finely chopped

1 carrot, peeled and
   finely chopped

1 fennel bulb, finely chopped

1 pound fresh mushrooms,
   quartered

8 cups Vegetable Broth
   (page 28), Poultry Broth
   (page 29), or store bought

¼ cup dry sherry

1 teaspoon dried thyme

1 teaspoon garlic powder

½ teaspoon sea salt

⅛ teaspoon freshly ground
   black pepper

1. In your slow cooker, combine all the ingredients, mixing to combine.

2. Cover and set on low. Cook for 8 hours.

PER SERVING Calories: 71; Total Fat: 0g; Saturated Fat: 0g; Cholesterol: 0mg; Carbohydrates: 15g; Fiber: 3g; Protein: 3g; Sodium: 145mg; Potassium: 465mg

PRECOOKING TIP To make the soup a little more flavorful, sauté the onion and carrot in 1 tablespoon of olive oil, stirring occasionally, for about 5 minutes. Then, stir in the sherry and scrape any browned bits from the bottom of the pan with the side of the spoon. Add the contents of the pan to the other ingredients in the slow cooker.

Minestrone

SERVES 6 • **PREP TIME:** 15 MINUTES • **COOK TIME:** 9 HOURS

Minestrone is made with lots of fresh vegetables, so it's an excellent and super healthy soup to serve as a meal. This recipe calls for whole-wheat pasta, but you can leave it out entirely or replace it with some cooked quinoa if you're sensitive to wheat or gluten.

2 carrots, peeled and sliced

2 celery stalks, sliced

1 onion, chopped

2 cups green beans, chopped

1 (16-ounce) can crushed tomatoes

2 cups cooked kidney beans (page 34), rinsed

6 cups Poultry Broth (page 29), Vegetable Broth (page 28), or store bought

1 teaspoon garlic powder

1 teaspoon dried Italian seasoning

¼ teaspoon sea salt

¼ teaspoon freshly ground black pepper

1½ cups cooked whole-wheat elbow macaroni (or pasta shape of your choice)

1 zucchini, chopped

1. In your slow cooker, combine the carrots, celery, onion, green beans, tomatoes, kidney beans, broth, garlic powder, Italian seasoning, salt, and pepper in the slow cooker.

2. Cover and cook on low for 8 hours.

3. Stir in the macaroni and zucchini. Cover and cook on low for 1 hour more.

PER SERVING Calories: 193; Total Fat: 0g; Saturated Fat: 0g; Cholesterol: 1mg; Carbohydrates: 39g; Fiber: 10g; Protein: 10g; Sodium: 267mg; Potassium: 893mg

Butternut Squash Soup

SERVES 6 • **PREP TIME:** 15 MINUTES • **COOK TIME:** 8 HOURS

This slightly sweet and earthy soup is the perfect meal for a cool fall or winter evening. If you'd like to make the soup vegan, simply replace the fat-free half-and-half with canned light coconut milk, which adds a tasty sweetness to the soup. This recipe will also work with acorn squash or sweet potatoes, so feel free to mix it up and make your own delicious variations.

1 butternut squash, peeled, seeded, and diced

1 onion, chopped

1 sweet-tart apple (such as Braeburn), peeled, cored, and chopped

3 cups Vegetable Broth (page 28), or store bought

1 teaspoon garlic powder

½ teaspoon ground sage

¼ teaspoon sea salt

¼ teaspoon freshly ground black pepper

Pinch cayenne pepper

Pinch nutmeg

½ cup fat-free half-and-half

1. In your slow cooker, combine the squash, onion, apple, broth, garlic powder, sage, salt, black pepper, cayenne, and nutmeg.

2. Cover and cook on low for 8 hours.

3. Using an immersion blender, counter-top blender, or food processor, purée the soup, adding the half-and-half as you do. Stir to combine, and serve.

A BALANCED MEAL Serve with a side salad and some whole-grain crackers to add grains and extra vegetables to your meal.

PER SERVING Calories: 106; Total Fat: 0g; Saturated Fat: 0g; Cholesterol: 0mg; Carbohydrates: 26g; Fiber: 4g; Protein: 3g; Sodium: 106mg; Potassium: 812mg

Pumpkin Soup

SERVES 6 · **PREP TIME:** 5 MINUTES · **COOK TIME:** 8 HOURS
Super Quick Prep

Pumpkin gives this soup a rich, earthy flavor and hearty texture that make it perfect for either lunch or dinner. The soup freezes well, so you can make a large batch in advance and store it, tightly sealed, in the freezer for up to 1 year. Be sure to buy canned pure pumpkin, not pumpkin pie filling.

1 (29-ounce) can pumpkin purée

2 carrots, peeled and chopped

1 onion, chopped

5 cups Vegetable Broth (page 28), or store bought

1 (14-ounce) can light coconut milk

1 teaspoon garlic powder

1 teaspoon onion powder

1 teaspoon ground cumin

½ teaspoon sea salt

¼ teaspoon freshly ground black pepper

3 tablespoons toasted pumpkin seeds (optional)

1 tablespoon chopped fresh chives (optional)

1. In your slow cooker, combine the pumpkin purée, carrots, onion, broth, coconut milk, garlic powder, onion powder, cumin, salt, and pepper.

2. Cover and cook on low for 8 hours.

3. Purée with an immersion blender.

4. Serve sprinkled with pumpkin seeds and chives, if desired.

PER SERVING Calories: 264; Total Fat: 18g; Saturated Fat: 14g; Cholesterol: 0mg; Carbohydrates: 24g; Fiber: 6g; Protein: 4g; Sodium: 104mg; Potassium: 687mg

Lentil Soup

SERVES 6 • **PREP TIME:** 10 MINUTES • **COOK TIME:** 8 HOURS
Super Quick Prep

Lentils make a hearty, high-protein meal. Many people cook lentil soup with a ham hock to get a smoky flavor. This one loses the salty ham hock and instead uses a dash of liquid smoke, which you can find in the spice aisle at the grocery store. With liquid smoke, a little goes a long way, so don't overdo it.

1 pound dried lentils, soaked overnight and rinsed

3 carrots, peeled and chopped

1 celery stalk, chopped

1 onion, chopped

6 cups Vegetable Broth (page 28), Poultry Broth (page 29), Beef Broth (page 30), or store bought

1½ teaspoons garlic powder

1 teaspoon ground cumin

1 teaspoon smoked paprika

1 teaspoon dried thyme

¼ teaspoon liquid smoke

¼ teaspoon sea salt

¼ teaspoon freshly ground black pepper

1. In your slow cooker, combine the lentils with all the other ingredients.

2. Cover and cook on low for 8 hours. Stir and serve.

PER SERVING Calories: 307; Total Fat: 1g; Saturated Fat: 0g; Cholesterol: 0mg; Carbohydrates: 56g; Fiber: 25g; Protein: 20g; Sodium: 124mg; Potassium: 999mg

A BALANCED MEAL Serve this soup with a simple side salad to add more vegetables to your meal. You can also add a dollop of fat-free sour cream on top of the soup to add some dairy.

Black Bean Soup

SERVES 6 • **PREP TIME:** 10 MINUTES • **COOK TIME:** 8 HOURS
Super Quick Prep

Just before you serve this soup, use a potato masher to mash the beans or purée the soup in a blender or food processor. The result is a hearty, smoky, spicy soup that is made even more delicious with the optional garnishes. It's great by itself as a meal, and it freezes well, so feel free to double the batch and put some away for a quick meal when you're in a hurry.

1 pound dried black beans, soaked overnight and rinsed

1 onion, chopped

1 carrot, peeled and chopped

2 jalapeño peppers, seeded and diced

6 cups Vegetable Broth (page 28), or store bought

1 teaspoon ground cumin

1 teaspoon ground coriander

1 teaspoon chili powder

½ teaspoon ground chipotle pepper (or more to taste)

½ teaspoon sea salt

¼ teaspoon freshly ground black pepper

Pinch cayenne pepper

¼ cup fat-free sour cream, for garnish (optional)

¼ cup grated low-fat Cheddar cheese, for garnish (optional)

1. In your slow cooker, combine all the ingredients.
2. Cover and cook on low for 8 hours.
3. If you'd like, mash the beans with a potato masher, or purée using an immersion blender, blender, or food processor.
4. Serve topped with the optional garnishes, if desired.

PRECOOKING TIP Soak the black beans in water for 8 to 12 hours before using them. Drain the beans, rinse them, then drain again before adding them to the slow cooker.

PER SERVING Calories: 320; Total Fat: 3g; Saturated Fat: 1g; Cholesterol: 6mg; Carbohydrates: 57g; Fiber: 13g; Protein: 18g; Sodium: 312mg; Potassium: 1332mg

Chickpea & Kale Soup

SERVES 6 • **PREP TIME:** 10 MINUTES • **COOK TIME:** 9 HOURS
Super Quick Prep

This hearty soup is chock-full of tasty vegetables, including kale, zucchini, and summer squash. Cooking kale in a slow cooker all day can leave your house smelling funky, so let the soup simmer for 8 hours, and then stir in the kale for the last hour to keep it tasting a bit fresher and to preserve its deep green color.

1 summer squash, quartered lengthwise and sliced crosswise

1 zucchini, quartered lengthwise and sliced crosswise

2 cups cooked chickpeas (page 34), rinsed

1 cup uncooked quinoa

2 (14-ounce) cans diced tomatoes, with their juice

5 cups Vegetable Broth (page 28), Poultry Broth (page 29), or store bought

1 teaspoon garlic powder

1 teaspoon onion powder

1 teaspoon dried thyme

½ teaspoon sea salt

2 cups chopped kale leaves

1. In your slow cooker, combine the summer squash, zucchini, chickpeas, quinoa, tomatoes (with their juice), broth, garlic powder, onion powder, thyme, and salt.

2. Cover and cook on low for 8 hours.

3. Stir in the kale. Cover and cook on low for 1 more hour.

PER SERVING Calories: 221; Total Fat: 3g; Saturated Fat: 0g; Cholesterol: 0mg; Carbohydrates: 40g; Fiber: 7g; Protein: 10g; Sodium: 200mg; Potassium: 1132mg

Clam Chowder

SERVES 6 • **PREP TIME:** 15 MINUTES • **COOK TIME:** 8 HOURS

This Manhattan-style clam chowder is creamy and a little bit smoky. The anise flavor of the fennel bulb and fronds makes an unusual and tasty addition that works well with the sweet clams. Garnishing with turkey bacon adds a perfect hint of smokiness that makes this chowder full of flavor and satisfying.

1 red onion, chopped

3 carrots, peeled and chopped

1 fennel bulb and fronds, chopped

1 (10-ounce) can chopped clams, with their juice

1 pound baby red potatoes, quartered

4 cups Poultry Broth (page 29), or store bought

½ teaspoon sea salt

⅛ teaspoon freshly ground black pepper

2 cups skim milk

¼ pound turkey bacon, browned and crumbled, for garnish

1. In your slow cooker, combine the onion, carrots, fennel bulb and fronds, clams (with their juice), potatoes, broth, salt, and pepper.

2. Cover and cook on low for 8 hours.

3. Stir in the milk and serve garnished with the crumbled bacon.

PER SERVING Calories: 172; Total Fat: 1g; Saturated Fat: 0g; Cholesterol: 14mg; Carbohydrates: 29g; Fiber: 4g; Protein: 10g; Sodium: 577mg; Potassium: 912mg

PRECOOKING TIP To incorporate the smoky flavor of the bacon into the chowder, cook it in 1 tablespoon of olive oil, and then add the onion, carrots, and fennel. Cook, stirring occasionally, until the vegetables begin to brown, about 5 minutes. Add to the slow cooker with the remaining ingredients.

Chicken & Rice Soup

SERVES 6 • **PREP TIME:** 10 MINUTES • **COOK TIME:** 8 HOURS
Super Quick Prep

Chicken, rice, and vegetables make this a balanced meal in a bowl. While this recipe calls for you to add 2 cups of cooked rice to the completed soup, you can instead add ¾ cup uncooked brown rice to the slow cooker and let it cook with the soup. This recipe keeps well and will freeze for up to 1 year.

1 pound boneless, skinless chicken thighs, cut into 1-inch pieces

1 onion, chopped

3 carrots, peeled and sliced

2 celery stalks, sliced

6 cups Poultry Broth (page 29), or store bought

1 teaspoon garlic powder

1 teaspoon dried rosemary

¼ teaspoon sea salt

¼ teaspoon freshly ground black pepper

3 cups cooked Brown Rice (page 31)

1. In your slow cooker, combine the chicken, onion, carrots, celery, broth, garlic powder, rosemary, salt, and pepper.

2. Cover and cook on low for 8 hours.

3. Stir in the rice about 10 minutes before serving, and allow the broth to warm it.

PER SERVING Calories: 354; Total Fat: 7g; Saturated Fat: 2g; Cholesterol: 67mg; Carbohydrates: 43g; Fiber: 3g; Protein: 28g; Sodium: 191mg; Potassium: 572mg

Tom Kha Gai

SERVES 6 • **PREP TIME:** 10 MINUTES • **COOK TIME:** 8 HOURS
Super Quick Prep

This tasty, fragrant soup features chicken and shiitake mushrooms in a flavorful coconut broth. It's wonderfully appetizing to come home from work and smell this soup simmering in your food processor. Asian fish sauce is made from fish (usually anchovies), salt, and water. Find it in the Asian food aisle in some supermarkets, or in Asian grocery stores or online.

1 pound boneless, skinless chicken thighs, cut into 1-inch pieces

1 pound fresh shiitake mushrooms, halved

2 tablespoons grated fresh ginger

3 cups canned light coconut milk

3 cups Poultry Broth (page 29), or store bought

1 tablespoon Asian fish sauce

1 teaspoon garlic powder

¼ teaspoon freshly ground black pepper

Juice of 1 lime

2 tablespoons chopped fresh cilantro

1. In your slow cooker, combine the chicken thighs, mushrooms, ginger, coconut milk, broth, fish sauce, garlic powder, and pepper.

2. Cover and cook on low for 8 hours.

3. Stir in the lime juice and cilantro just before serving.

PER SERVING Calories: 481; Total Fat: 35g; Saturated Fat: 27g; Cholesterol: 67mg; Carbohydrates: 19g; Fiber: 5g; Protein: 28g; Sodium: 604mg; Potassium: 827mg

A BALANCED MEAL To add some vegetables and grains, chop up 3 carrots and add them to the soup as it cooks, then serve with ½ cup brown rice per serving. You can also substitute shrimp or chopped tofu for the chicken, although it's best to add cooked shrimp about 30 minutes before serving and allow them to warm in the broth, rather than adding them at the beginning of cooking.

Chicken Corn Chowder

SERVES 6 • **PREP TIME:** 10 MINUTES • **COOK TIME:** 8 HOURS
Super Quick Prep

If you enjoy spicy, Southwestern-style flavors, you'll love this chicken and corn chowder. Jalapeño peppers give it lots of zip. To lessen the impact and heat of the peppers, be sure to carefully remove the seeds and ribs before dicing them. Or, feel free to leave the seeds in to really turn up the heat.

1 pound boneless, skinless chicken thighs, cut into 1-inch pieces

2 onions, chopped

3 jalapeño peppers, seeded and minced

2 red bell peppers, seeded and chopped

1½ cups fresh or frozen corn

6 cups Poultry Broth (page 29), or store bought

1 teaspoon garlic powder

½ teaspoon sea salt

¼ teaspoon freshly ground black pepper

1 cup skim milk

1. In your slow cooker, combine the chicken, onions, jalapeños, red bell peppers, corn, broth, garlic powder, salt, and pepper.

2. Cover and cook on low for 8 hours.

3. Stir in the skim milk just before serving.

PRECOOKING TIP To add flavor, brown the chicken, onions, jalapeños, and bell peppers in 2 tablespoons of olive oil, for about 5 minutes before adding them to the slow cooker.

PER SERVING Calories: 236; Total Fat: 6g; Saturated Fat: 2g; Cholesterol: 68mg; Carbohydrates: 17g; Fiber: 3g; Protein: 27g; Sodium: 634mg; Potassium: 754mg

Turkey Ginger Soup

SERVES 6 • **PREP TIME:** 10 MINUTES • **COOK TIME:** 8 HOURS
Super Quick Prep

This tasty soup has a bright Asian flavor that's really delicious. Fragrant with garlic, ginger, and sesame oil, and brimming with delicious lean turkey and rice, it's a perfect hearty lunch or dinner. It stores well in the freezer, so make a double batch. Toasted sesame oil has a big, smoky taste and is used as a flavoring; find it in the Asian foods aisle of your supermarket.

1 pound boneless, skinless turkey thighs, cut into 1-inch pieces

1 pound fresh shiitake mushrooms, halved

3 carrots, peeled and sliced

2 cups frozen peas

1 tablespoon grated fresh ginger

6 cups Poultry Broth (page 29), or store bought

1 tablespoon low-sodium soy sauce

1 teaspoon toasted sesame oil

2 teaspoons garlic powder

1½ cups cooked Brown Rice (page 31)

1. In your slow cooker, combine the turkey, mushrooms, carrots, peas, ginger, broth, soy sauce, sesame oil, and garlic powder.

2. Cover and cook on low for 8 hours.

3. About 30 minutes before serving, stir in the rice to warm it through.

PRECOOKING TIP To infuse even more ginger, add 5 or 6 slices of fresh ginger to the slow cooker when you make your poultry broth. Use this gingery broth for this soup and the Tom Kha Gai (page 47).

PER SERVING Calories: 318; Total Fat: 7g; Saturated Fat: 0g; Cholesterol: 0mg; Carbohydrates: 42g; Fiber: 6g; Protein: 24g; Sodium: 532mg; Potassium: 712mg

Italian Wedding Soup

SERVES 6 • **PREP TIME:** 15 MINUTES • **COOK TIME:** 7 TO 8 HOURS

Italian wedding soup is an Italian-American classic. The term "wedding soup" is a mistranslation of the Italian phrase *minestra maritata* or "married soup." It means that the tasty little meatballs go well simmered in broth with the greens—a perfect marriage of flavors. This soup gives you plenty of protein and a healthy serving of green vegetables. Because you don't want to overcook the greens, stir them into the soup about an hour before serving. This will cook them without turning them to mush.

1 pound ground turkey breast

1½ cups cooked Brown Rice (page 31)

1 onion, grated

¼ cup chopped fresh parsley

1 egg, beaten

1 teaspoon garlic powder

1 teaspoon sea salt, divided

6 cups Poultry Broth (page 29), or store bought

⅛ teaspoon freshly ground black pepper

Pinch red pepper flakes

1 pound kale, tough stems removed, leaves chopped

1. In a small bowl, combine the turkey breast, rice, onion, parsley, egg, garlic powder, and ½ teaspoon of sea salt.

2. Roll the mixture into ½-inch meatballs and put them in the slow cooker.

3. Add the broth, black pepper, red pepper flakes, and the remaining ½ teaspoon of sea salt.

4. Cover and cook on low for 7 to 8 hours.

5. An hour before serving, stir in the kale. Cover and cook until the kale wilts.

PRECOOKING TIP For even more flavor, brown the meat-balls in 2 tablespoons olive oil for about 5 minutes before you add them to the slow cooker.

PER SERVING Calories: 302; Total Fat: 7g; Saturated Fat: 2g; Cholesterol: 83mg; Carbohydrates: 29g; Fiber: 3g; Protein: 29g; Sodium: 528mg; Potassium: 912mg

Taco Soup

SERVES 6 • **PREP TIME:** 15 MINUTES • **COOK TIME:** 8 HOURS

If you like all the flavors that come in tacos, then you'll love this soup. Brown your ground turkey ahead of time for best results. It will cook if you put it raw in the soup, but it sometimes clumps up into tiny meatballs. Browning beforehand makes this less of an issue. This soup has lots of spicy flavor, and it's fragrant and tasty.

1 pound ground turkey breast

1 onion, chopped

1 (14-ounce) can tomatoes and green chiles, with their juice

6 cups Poultry Broth (page 29), or store bought

1 teaspoon chili powder

1 teaspoon ground cumin

½ teaspoon sea salt

¼ cup chopped fresh cilantro

Juice of 1 lime

½ cup grated low-fat Cheddar cheese

1. Crumble the turkey into the slow cooker.

2. Add the onion, tomatoes and green chiles (with their juice), broth, chili power, cumin, and salt.

3. Cover and cook on low for 8 hours.

4. Stir in the cilantro and lime juice.

5. Serve garnished with the cheese.

PER SERVING Calories: 281; Total Fat: 10g; Saturated Fat: 4g; Cholesterol: 66mg; Carbohydrates: 20g; Fiber: 5g; Protein: 30g; Sodium: 372mg; Potassium: 649mg

Italian Sausage & Fennel Soup

SERVES 6 • **PREP TIME:** 10 MINUTES • **COOK TIME:** 8 HOURS
Super Quick Prep

Using chicken or turkey sausage makes this soup a lot leaner. Choose sausage that comes in casings, not bulk sausage (loose sausage meat), because casings will help the sausage hold its shape in the slow cooker. Fennel, a cousin to anise and licorice flavor-wise, is a classic to pair with Italian sausage, and it gives this soup a memorable savoriness.

1 pound Italian chicken
or turkey sausage,
cut into ½-inch slices

2 onions, chopped

1 fennel bulb, chopped

6 cups Poultry Broth (page 29),
or store bought

¼ cup dry sherry

1½ teaspoons garlic powder

1 teaspoon dried thyme

½ teaspoon sea salt

¼ teaspoon freshly ground
black pepper

Pinch red pepper flakes

1. In your slow cooker, combine all the ingredients.

2. Cover and cook on low for 8 hours.

PER SERVING Calories: 311; Total Fat: 22g; Saturated Fat: 7g; Cholesterol: 64mg; Carbohydrates: 8g; Fiber: 2g; Protein: 18g; Sodium: 844mg; Potassium: 646mg

Beef & Barley Soup

SERVES 6 • **PREP TIME:** 10 MINUTES • **COOK TIME:** 8 HOURS
Super Quick Prep

Beef and barley is a classic soup combo that gives you a hearty serving of protein and grains. If you have time, brown the ground beef on the stove top so it doesn't clump together. You can also use any cut of lean beef, such as grass-fed stew meat, or substitute ground turkey or chicken.

1 pound extra-lean ground beef

2 onions, chopped

3 carrots, peeled and sliced

1 pound fresh mushrooms, quartered

1½ cups dried barley

6 cups Beef Broth (page 30), or store bought

1 teaspoon ground mustard

1 teaspoon dried thyme

1 teaspoon garlic powder

¼ teaspoon sea salt

⅛ teaspoon freshly ground black pepper

1. In your slow cooker, crumble the ground beef into small pieces.
2. Add the remaining ingredients.
3. Cover and cook on low for 8 hours.

PER SERVING Calories: 319; Total Fat: 5g; Saturated Fat: 2g; Cholesterol: 40mg; Carbohydrates: 44g; Fiber: 11g; Protein: 28g; Sodium: 224mg; Potassium: 1114mg

SMART SHOPPING TIP Buying ground beef in bulk can save you money. To save time on busy mornings, buy a large amount of extra-lean ground beef and brown it. Freeze 1-pound portions in resealable bags for up to 1 year.

Stews, Curries & Chilies

Sweet Potato Curry with Lentils

SERVES 4 • **PREP TIME:** 10 MINUTES • **COOK TIME:** 8 HOURS
Super Quick Prep

This hearty vegetarian dish just gets better the longer it simmers in the slow cooker—it's even tastier the next day if you refrigerate and reheat the leftovers. This recipe also freezes well, so it's a good one to double up on in order to make tasty meals on the go.

4 sweet potatoes, peeled and cut into 1-inch cubes

1 onion, chopped

1 cup dried green lentils, soaked overnight and rinsed

1 (14-ounce) can chopped tomatoes, with their juice

1 cup canned light coconut milk

1 cup Vegetable Broth (page 28), or store bought

1 tablespoon curry powder

1 teaspoon garlic powder

½ teaspoon sea salt

2 tablespoons chopped fresh cilantro

1. In your slow cooker, combine the sweet potatoes, onion, lentils, tomatoes (with their juice), coconut milk, broth, curry powder, garlic powder, and salt.

2. Cover and cook on low for 8 hours.

3. Stir in the cilantro and serve.

PER SERVING Calories: 525; Total Fat: 16g; Saturated Fat: 13g; Cholesterol: 0mg; Carbohydrates: 83g; Fiber: 25g; Protein: 18g; Sodium: 182mg; Potassium: 1844mg

Chicken & Root Vegetable Stew

SERVES 6 • **PREP TIME:** 15 MINUTES • **COOK TIME:** 8 HOURS

Boneless, skinless chicken thighs hold up fairly well in the slow cooker because they have a little bit of fat running through the meat. If you'd like your stew leaner, just replace them with 1 pound boneless, skinless chicken breasts. The texture of the meat will be slightly drier and stringier, but it still makes a delicious stew.

3 cups Poultry Broth (page 29), or store bought

2 tablespoons cornstarch

1 pound boneless, skinless chicken thighs, cut into 1-inch pieces

4 carrots, peeled and cut into ½-inch pieces

2 red onions, chopped

1 pound red potatoes, scrubbed and cut into 1-inch pieces

1 fennel bulb, chopped

3 garlic cloves, minced

½ cup dry white wine

1 teaspoon dried thyme

½ teaspoon sea salt

¼ teaspoon freshly ground black pepper

1. In a small bowl, whisk together the broth and cornstarch.
2. Add the mixture to the slow cooker, along with all the remaining ingredients.
3. Cover and cook on low for 8 hours.

PER SERVING Calories: 277; Total Fat: 6g; Saturated Fat: 2g; Cholesterol: 67mg; Carbohydrates: 26g; Fiber: 4g; Protein: 26g; Sodium: 277mg; Potassium: 901mg

SMART SHOPPING TIP To save money, you can buy skin-on, bone-in chicken thighs and remove the skin and bones yourself using a boning knife (a thin knife with a curved, tapered blade) or poultry shears.

Chicken & Sweet Potato Curry

SERVES 6 • **PREP TIME:** 15 MINUTES • **COOK TIME:** 8 HOURS

This rich curry is warming and delicious—and super easy in a slow cooker. Light coconut milk keeps saturated fat and calories low, and the curry powder and spices add plenty of flavor. Be sure you use a curry powder purchased in the spice aisle, and not a prepackaged curry mix that has salt added. Read the label before you buy, just to be sure. It's important to control the amount of salt in the recipe to keep it DASH-friendly.

1 pound boneless, skinless chicken thighs, cut into 1-inch pieces

2 sweet potatoes, peeled and cut into 1-inch cubes

2 red bell peppers, seeded and cut into large pieces

1 onion, chopped

2 cups Poultry Broth (page 29), or store bought

1 cup canned light coconut milk

2 teaspoons curry powder

1 teaspoon garlic powder

½ teaspoon sea salt

¼ teaspoon freshly ground black pepper

1. In your slow cooker, combine all the ingredients.

2. Cover and cook on low for 8 hours.

PER SERVING Calories: 323; Total Fat: 16g; Saturated Fat: 10g; Cholesterol: 67mg; Carbohydrates: 21g; Fiber: 4g; Protein: 25g; Sodium: 234mg; Potassium: 824mg

A BALANCED MEAL Add more vegetables to this curry by adding 2 cups chopped cauliflower to the slow cooker before cooking. Additionally, add 1 chopped zucchini to the slow cooker 1 hour before serving.

Chicken Tikka Masala

SERVES 6 • **PREP TIME:** 10 MINUTES • **COOK TIME:** 8 HOURS
Super Quick Prep

Tikka masala is a curry dish that benefits from slow cooking, because the longer the cook time, the more the flavors build. Use boneless, skinless thighs in this recipe, because they'll hold up better than breasts for the long cooking time. Garam masala is a blend of ground spices available at most supermarkets and online.

1 pound boneless, skinless chicken thighs, cut into 1-inch pieces

2 onions, chopped

1 teaspoon garlic powder

1 teaspoon grated fresh ginger

1 (28-ounce) can diced tomatoes, drained

1 cup canned light coconut milk

½ teaspoon Asian fish sauce

2 tablespoons garam masala

¼ cup chopped fresh cilantro

3 cups cooked Brown Rice (page 31)

1. In your slow cooker, combine the chicken, onions, garlic powder, ginger, tomatoes, coconut milk, fish sauce, and garam masala.

2. Cover and cook on low for 8 hours.

3. Stir in the cilantro and serve over the cooked brown rice.

PER SERVING Calories: 450; Total Fat: 18g; Saturated Fat: 10g; Cholesterol: 67mg; Carbohydrates: 48g; Fiber: 5g; Protein: 28g; Sodium: 124mg; Potassium: 797mg

PRECOOKING TIP Make your own garam masala by mixing 1 tablespoon ground cumin, 1½ teaspoons ground coriander, 1½ teaspoons ground cardamom, 1½ teaspoons freshly ground black pepper, 1 teaspoon ground cinnamon, ½ teaspoon ground nutmeg, and ½ teaspoon ground cloves. Keep it tightly sealed in your spice cupboard.

Coq au Vin

SERVES 6 • **PREP TIME:** 15 MINUTES • **COOK TIME:** 8 HOURS

Coq au vin is a classic French dish braised in wine. Originally, the dish was created to tenderize an old rooster, and braising suited this purpose beautifully. Here, you use skinless thighs to lower the fat content but still keep the chicken moist and tender. You can cook them with the bone in or out; it's up to you, but cooking with the bone in imparts more flavor.

6 bone-in, skinless chicken thighs

4 slices turkey bacon, browned and crumbled

2 cups frozen pearl onions

1 pound fresh mushrooms, quartered

3 carrots, peeled and sliced

1½ cups dry red wine

2 cups Poultry Broth (page 29), or store bought

1 teaspoon garlic powder

1 teaspoon dried thyme

½ teaspoon sea salt

¼ teaspoon freshly ground black pepper

¼ cup chopped fresh parsley

1. In your slow cooker, combine the chicken, bacon, pearl onions, mushrooms, carrots, wine, broth, garlic powder, thyme, salt, and pepper.

2. Cover and cook on low for 8 hours.

3. Stir in the parsley just before serving.

PRECOOKING TIP Brown the chicken in 2 tablespoons olive oil in a sauté pan for about 5 minutes before adding it to the slow cooker. Then, while the pan is still on the heat, add the red wine and scrape any browned bits from the bottom of the pan. Add the wine to the slow cooker. This adds tremendous flavor.

PER SERVING Calories: 234; Total Fat: 6g; Saturated Fat: 4g; Cholesterol: 77mg; Carbohydrates: 11g; Fiber: 2g; Protein: 31g; Sodium: 131mg; Potassium: 388mg

Spicy Southwestern Chicken Stew

SERVES 6 • **PREP TIME:** 10 MINUTES • **COOK TIME:** 8 HOURS
Super Quick Prep

Jalapeños give this stew a nice dash of heat without being overwhelming. Using canned diced jalapeños also saves time, although you can feel free to substitute 2 chopped fresh jalapeños, if you wish. Serve it over cooked rice and topped with some low-fat grated cheese for a hearty, balanced meal.

2 cups Poultry Broth (page 29), or store bought

1 tablespoon cornstarch

1 pound boneless, skinless chicken thighs, cut into 1-inch pieces

2 onions, chopped

3 carrots, peeled and sliced

2 (4-ounce) cans chopped jalapeño peppers, with their juice

2 red bell peppers, seeded and chopped

2 cups fresh or frozen corn

¼ teaspoon sea salt

¼ cup chopped fresh cilantro

1. In a small bowl, whisk together the poultry broth and cornstarch.

2. Add the mixture to the slow cooker, along with the chicken, onions, carrots, jalapeños (and their juice), red bell peppers, corn, and salt.

3. Cover and cook on low for 8 hours.

4. Stir in the cilantro before serving.

PER SERVING Calories: 179; Total Fat: 5g; Saturated Fat: 3g; Cholesterol: 47mg; Carbohydrates: 20g; Fiber: 4g; Protein: 20g; Sodium: 800mg; Potassium: 615mg

White Bean & Chicken Chili

SERVES 4 • **PREP TIME:** 15 MINUTES • **COOK TIME:** 8 HOURS

White beans and chicken make a delicious low-fat, high-protein chili. The warming spices lend complexity, and the white beans and chicken act almost like sponges to pull in all the flavor. This is a chili that tastes even better the second day; consider making a double batch so you have leftovers to take for meals on the go. This chili also freezes well.

1 pound boneless, skinless chicken thighs, cut into 1-inch pieces

1 pound dried white beans, soaked overnight and rinsed

2 onions, chopped

2 green bell peppers, seeded and chopped

3 cups Poultry Broth (page 29), or store bought

1 tablespoon chili powder

2 teaspoons garlic powder

1 teaspoon ground cumin

¼ teaspoon sea salt

1. In your slow cooker, combine all the ingredients.

2. Cover and cook on low for 8 hours.

PER SERVING Calories: 562; Total Fat: 5g; Saturated Fat: 3g; Cholesterol: 70mg; Carbohydrates: 80g; Fiber: 21g; Protein: 52g; Sodium: 257mg; Potassium: 2578mg

A BALANCED MEAL
Garnish each bowl of chili with 2 tablespoons low-fat cheese, 1 tablespoon fat-free sour cream, and one-quarter of a diced avocado.

Chicken Stew with Peas, Carrots & Pearl Onions

SERVES 6 • **PREP TIME:** 15 MINUTES • **COOK TIME:** 8 HOURS

This dish calls for pearl onions. If you buy them fresh, you'll need to peel them. To do so, blanch them for three minutes in boiling water, plunge them into ice water, and then peel away the exterior. To save time, you can also use frozen pearl onions, which are already peeled.

6 chicken hindquarters

8 ounces baby carrots

8 ounces fresh or frozen pearl onions

4 cups vegetable broth

2 cups dry white wine

1 bay leaf

1 teaspoon dried tarragon

½ teaspoon salt

⅛ teaspoon black pepper

2 cups peas (fresh or frozen)

¼ cup chopped fresh parsley

1. In your slow cooker, combine the chicken, baby carrots, onion, broth, wine, bay leaf, tarragon, salt, and pepper.

2. Cover and cook on low for 7½ hours.

3. Stir in the peas. Cover and cook for an additional 30 minutes.

4. Stir in the parsley just before serving.

PER SERVING (1 Cup) Calories: 307; Total Fat: 6g; Saturated Fat: 2g; Cholesterol: 81mg; Carbohydrates: 15g; Fiber 4g; Protein: 32g; Sodium: 362mg; Potassium: 783mg

Southwestern Chili

SERVES 6 • **PREP TIME:** 10 MINUTES • **COOK TIME:** 8 HOURS
Super Quick Prep

This is a classic Southwestern chili, although it uses ground turkey breast rather than ground beef, to lower the fat. You can make it spicier by adding cayenne pepper as it cooks, but remember, a little goes a long way. Start with about ⅛ teaspoon and test the heat before adding more. Also bear in mind that the heat intensifies over time, so the next day's leftovers will taste a bit hotter than the chili that comes right out of the slow cooker.

1 pound ground turkey breast

3 cups cooked kidney beans (page 34), rinsed

1 onion, chopped

2 (14-ounce) cans crushed tomatoes

2 tablespoons chili powder

2 teaspoons garlic powder

1 teaspoon dried oregano

½ teaspoon ground cumin

½ teaspoon sea salt

Pinch cayenne pepper (optional)

1. Crumble the ground turkey breast into small pieces in your slow cooker.

2. Add the cooked kidney beans, onion, tomatoes, chili powder, garlic powder, oregano, cumin, salt, and cayenne (if using).

3. Cover and cook on low for 8 hours.

A BALANCED MEAL Serve this chili over ¼ cup cooked brown rice to add grains, and garnish with chopped tomatoes, scallions, and avocados to add more vegetables to the meal.

PER SERVING Calories: 328; Total Fat: 7g; Saturated Fat: 2g; Cholesterol: 56mg; Carbohydrates: 35g; Fiber: 12g; Protein: 33g; Sodium: 490mg; Potassium: 935mg

Classic Beef Stew

SERVES 6 • **PREP TIME:** 15 MINUTES • **COOK TIME:** 8 HOURS

Stew beef cuts include chuck roast and similar tough cuts. While these are fattier cuts, taking the time to skim the fat reduces the overall fat content. You should also trim away any large chunks of fat before cooking, but leave the marbling in the meat. This will result in a tender stew that isn't terribly fatty. Browned turkey bacon adds a delicious, low-fat, smoky note to the stew.

2 cups Beef Broth (page 30), or store bought

1 tablespoon cornstarch

1 pound stew beef, trimmed and cut into 1-inch cubes

4 slices turkey bacon, browned and crumbled

4 carrots, peeled and chopped

1 pound red potatoes, scrubbed and chopped

1 pound fresh mushrooms, halved

½ cup red wine

1 tablespoon ground mustard

1 teaspoon dried rosemary

¼ teaspoon sea salt

¼ teaspoon freshly ground black pepper

1. In a small bowl, whisk together the broth and cornstarch.
2. Add the mixture to your slow cooker, along with the remaining ingredients.
3. Cover and cook on low for 8 hours.
4. Skim any excess fat from the surface and discard.

PER SERVING Calories: 244; Total Fat: 6g; Saturated Fat: 0g; Cholesterol: 7mg; Carbohydrates: 21g; Fiber: 3g; Protein: 24g; Sodium: 196mg; Potassium: 750mg

PRECOOKING TIP To add deeper flavor to this stew, brown the meat in 2 tablespoons olive oil for about 3 minutes per side. Pour the wine into the pan and scrape any browned bits from the bottom with the side of your spoon before adding it to the slow cooker.

Vietnamese Beef Stew

SERVES 6 • **PREP TIME:** 15 MINUTES • **COOK TIME:** 8 HOURS

This slightly sweet, slightly spicy stew has a delicious Asian flavor profile that's positively addictive. It perfectly balances the salty fish sauce and sweet honey with the aromatics of the Chinese five-spice powder. If you can't find five-spice powder at your grocery store, you can make your own (see the Smart Shopping Tip below). One of the ingredients, Szechuan pepper, is fragrant and not hot at all, but it does make your lips tingle a bit when used on its own.

2 cups Beef Broth (page 30), or store bought

1 tablespoon cornstarch

1 pound stew beef, trimmed and cut into 1-inch cubes

3 carrots, peeled and chopped

1 onion, sliced

1 (14-ounce) can crushed tomatoes, with their juice

1 tablespoon honey

1 teaspoon Asian fish sauce

1 tablespoon five-spice powder

1 teaspoon garlic powder

¼ teaspoon freshly ground black pepper

1. In a small bowl, whisk together the broth and cornstarch.
2. Add the mixture to your slow cooker, along with the remaining ingredients.
3. Cover and cook on low for 8 hours.

PER SERVING Calories: 187; Total Fat: 5g; Saturated Fat: 0g; Cholesterol: 0mg; Carbohydrates: 15g; Fiber: 4g; Protein: 20g; Sodium: 226mg; Potassium: 135mg

SMART SHOPPING TIP Make your own Chinese five-spice powder by combining 1 teaspoon ground cinnamon, 1 teaspoon ground cloves, 1 teaspoon ground fennel seeds, 1 teaspoon ground star anise, and 1 teaspoon ground Szechuan pepper.

Curried Beef

SERVES 6 • **PREP TIME:** 10 MINUTES • **COOK TIME:** 8 HOURS

This beefy curry comes in a hearty tomato broth that is fragrant with curry and spices. Trim the beef of excess fat before cooking it, and be sure to skim away excess fat before serving, to lower the fat content of this dish. While the recipe calls for stew meat, you can also use chuck roast cut into cubes and trimmed of excess fat.

1 pound stew beef, trimmed and cut into 1-inch pieces

2 (15-ounce) cans diced tomatoes, with their juice

1 pound red potatoes, scrubbed and cut into 1-inch pieces

1 onion, sliced

4 large carrots, peeled and cut into 1-inch pieces

1 tablespoon grated fresh ginger

2 tablespoons curry powder

1 teaspoon ground cumin

1 teaspoon garlic powder

½ teaspoon sea salt

1. In your slow cooker, combine all the ingredients.

2. Cover and cook on low for 8 hours.

3. Using a large spoon, skim the fat from the surface of the curry and discard.

A BALANCED MEAL Stir in 2 cups of torn spinach leaves an hour before you finish cooking the curry, to add some greens to this savory dish.

PER SERVING Calories: 229; Total Fat: 5g; Saturated Fat: 0g; Cholesterol: 0mg; Carbohydrates: 26g; Fiber: 6g; Protein: 20g; Sodium: 203mg; Potassium: 916mg

Hungarian Goulash

SERVES 6 • **PREP TIME:** 15 MINUTES • **COOK TIME:** 8 HOURS

Traditional Hungarian goulash is made with smoked paprika, for a savory, smoky flavor, but feel free to substitute any type of paprika you prefer—or blend sweet, hot, and smoked for a complex flavor profile. Traditionally, goulash is served over egg noodles, but serving it on cooked quinoa adds hearty whole grains to the dish.

2 cups Beef Broth (page 30), or store bought

1 tablespoon cornstarch

1 pound stew beef, trimmed and cut into 1-inch cubes

2 onions, sliced

3 carrots, peeled and sliced

¼ cup tomato paste

2 tablespoons smoked paprika

1 teaspoon garlic powder

½ teaspoon sea salt

3 cups cooked Quinoa (page 32)

1. In a small bowl, whisk together the broth and cornstarch.
2. Add the mixture to your slow cooker, along with the beef, onions, carrots, tomato paste, paprika, garlic powder, and salt. Stir to combine.
3. Cover and cook on low for 8 hours.
4. Skim any excess fat from the surface and discard.
5. Serve over the quinoa.

A BALANCED MEAL Add dairy to the goulash by stirring in 1 cup fat-free sour cream just before serving. Serve alongside steamed broccoli to make a balanced meal.

PER SERVING Calories: 321; Total Fat: 8g; Saturated Fat: 0g; Cholesterol: 0mg; Carbohydrates: 39g; Fiber: 6g; Protein: 25g; Sodium: 192mg; Potassium: 560mg

Pork, Fennel & Apple Stew

SERVES 6 • **PREP TIME:** 15 MINUTES • **COOK TIME:** 8 HOURS

Pork, fennel, apples, red onion, and mustard are a classic flavor combination that work beautifully in this dish. Before you cook a pork shoulder, be sure to remove the skin and as much visible fat as possible from the exterior of the cut. Leave the intramuscular fat to keep the pork tender, and then skim any excess fat from the stew with a spoon before serving.

1 pound pork shoulder, trimmed of as much fat as possible and cut into 1-inch cubes

2 sweet-tart apples (such as Braeburn), peeled, cored, and sliced

1 fennel bulb, sliced

2 red onions, sliced

¼ cup apple cider vinegar

2 cups Poultry Broth (page 29), or store bought

1 teaspoon garlic powder

1 teaspoon ground mustard

½ teaspoon ground cinnamon

½ teaspoon sea salt

⅛ teaspoon freshly ground black pepper

1. In your slow cooker, combine all the ingredients.

2. Cover and cook on low for 8 hours.

PER SERVING Calories: 297; Total Fat: 11g; Saturated Fat: 4g; Cholesterol: 76mg; Carbohydrates: 15g; Fiber: 4g; Protein: 21g; Sodium: 230mg; Potassium: 546mg

A BALANCED MEAL Serve with ¼ cup cooked Quinoa (page 32) per serving to add grains. If you'd like to pump up the vegetable content, add 2 cups shredded cabbage about an hour before serving and allow it to cook with the rest of the stew.

Moroccan Lamb Stew

SERVES 6 • **PREP TIME:** 15 MINUTES • **COOK TIME:** 8 HOURS

The slightly gamey taste of lamb lends itself beautifully to a blend of fragrant Moroccan spices. Be sure to trim as much fat as possible from the lamb shoulder, leaving a little bit of marbling in the meat to aid in the braising process. Serve on top of whole-wheat couscous for a balanced supper.

1 pound lamb shoulder, trimmed of fat and cut into 1-inch cubes

2 cup Poultry Broth (page 29) or Beef Broth (page 30), or store bought

1 pint cherry tomatoes

2 onions, sliced

1 tablespoon grated fresh ginger

2 teaspoons ground cumin

1 teaspoon garlic powder

½ teaspoon ground cinnamon

¼ teaspoon sea salt

¼ teaspoon freshly ground black pepper

3 cups cooked whole-wheat couscous

¼ cup chopped fresh cilantro

1. In your slow cooker, combine the lamb, broth, tomatoes, onions, ginger, cumin, garlic powder, cinnamon, salt, and pepper.

2. Cover and cook on low for 8 hours.

3. Skim any excess fat from the surface of the stew and discard.

4. Serve over the couscous. Garnish with the cilantro.

PER SERVING Calories: 353; Total Fat: 6g; Saturated Fat: 2g; Cholesterol: 68mg; Carbohydrates: 45g; Fiber: 5g; Protein: 28g; Sodium: 171mg; Potassium: 693mg

Irish Lamb Stew

SERVES 6 • **PREP TIME:** 15 MINUTES • **COOK TIME:** 8 HOURS

This stew combines lamb, barley, and root vegetables in a flavorful and hearty meal. Leeks can get a lot of dirt trapped between the layers, so be sure to wash them thoroughly. To do this, cut the leeks into pieces and put them in a large bowl of cold water. Use your hands to agitate the leeks and then let them sit for a few minutes so the dirt settles to the bottom of the bowl. Repeat this process, replacing the water and continuing until no dirt settles in the bottom of the bowl.

1 pound lamb leg, trimmed of fat and cut into 1-inch pieces

2 onions, sliced

2 leeks, chopped

4 large carrots, peeled and cut into 1-inch chunks

1 cup fresh or frozen peas

½ cup uncooked barley

3 cups Beef Broth (page 30), or store bought

1 tablespoon dried rosemary

1 teaspoon ground mustard

½ teaspoon sea salt

¼ teaspoon freshly ground black pepper

1. In your slow cooker, combine all the ingredients.

2. Cover and cook on low for 8 hours.

3. Skim any excess fat from the surface of the stew and discard.

PER SERVING Calories: 338; Total Fat: 18g; Saturated Fat: 8g; Cholesterol: 54mg; Carbohydrates: 28g; Fiber: 7g; Protein: 18g; Sodium: 275mg; Potassium: 622mg

PRECOOKING TIP Brown the lamb in a sauté pan with 1 to 2 tablespoons olive oil for better flavor. Cook for 3 to 4 minutes per side.

Vegetarian & Vegan Dishes

Eggplant & Chickpeas

SERVES 6 • **PREP TIME:** 15 MINUTES • **COOK TIME:** 8 HOURS

This slow cooker dish has a flavor profile similar to that of the Mediterranean dish moussaka. While traditional moussaka doesn't have chickpeas, this version does, to add some protein. Oregano, garlic, and cinnamon make for an interesting flavor combination that gives this dish its characteristic Greek flavor.

2 eggplants, peeled
  and chopped

2 cups cooked chickpeas
  (page 34), rinsed

2 onions, chopped

2 (14-ounce) cans
  crushed tomatoes

2 teaspoons garlic powder

1 teaspoon dried oregano

½ teaspoon sea salt

¼ teaspoon freshly ground
  black pepper

¼ teaspoon ground cinnamon

3 ounces low-fat feta cheese

1. In your slow cooker, combine the eggplant, chickpeas, onions, tomatoes, garlic powder, oregano, salt, pepper, and cinnamon.

2. Cover and cook on low for 8 hours.

3. Crumble the feta cheese over the top just before serving.

PER SERVING Calories: 191; Total Fat: 3g; Saturated Fat: 1g; Cholesterol: 5mg; Carbohydrates: 33g; Fiber: 13g; Protein: 11g; Sodium: 596mg; Potassium: 771mg

PRECOOKING TIP One way to make eggplant tastier is to remove the bitter liquid in the vegetable before using it. To do this, put the chopped eggplant in a colander and sprinkle it with salt. Leave it to sit and drain for about 30 minutes. Then rinse the eggplant well, pat dry with paper towels, and proceed with the recipe as written.

Chickpea Curry

SERVES 6 • **PREP TIME:** 10 MINUTES • **COOK TIME:** 9 HOURS
Super Quick Prep

Sweet potatoes add sweetness to the earthy flavor of the chickpeas. Because of their size and shape, dried chickpeas take a little longer to cook than other legumes, so you'll need to cook them for at least 9 hours to get them nice and tender. If you can't find dried chickpeas, feel free to use 2 (14-ounce) cans low-sodium chickpeas (rinsed and drained), but reduce the cooking time to 8 hours.

1 pound dried chickpeas, soaked overnight and rinsed

2 medium sweet potatoes, peeled and chopped

1 (14-ounce) can crushed tomatoes

8 scallions, chopped

7 cups Vegetable Broth (page 28), or store bought

2 tablespoons curry powder

1 teaspoon garlic powder

½ teaspoon sea salt

¼ teaspoon freshly ground black pepper

¼ cup chopped fresh cilantro

1. In your slow cooker, combine the chickpeas, sweet potatoes, tomatoes, scallions, broth, curry powder, garlic powder, salt, and pepper.

2. Cover and cook for 9 hours.

3. Stir in the cilantro just before serving.

A BALANCED MEAL Add 2 chopped red bell peppers at the start of cooking to add flavor and a serving of vegetables to this dish.

PER SERVING Calories: 394; Total Fat: 5g; Saturated Fat: 1g; Cholesterol: 0mg; Carbohydrates: 73g; Fiber: 19g; Protein: 18g; Sodium: 324mg; Potassium: 1390mg

Fava Beans

SERVES 12 • **PREP TIME:** 5 MINUTES • **COOK TIME:** 8 TO 10 HOURS
Super Quick Prep

Cooked fava beans make an excellent last-minute addition to soups, stews, and salads, as well as a fantastic snack or side dish. Store them in ½-cup portions in resealable bags in the freezer for up to 1 year. Thaw in the refrigerator overnight or in the microwave for 1 minute.

1 pound fava beans, soaked overnight and rinsed

1 tablespoon olive oil

1 teaspoon ground cumin

1 teaspoon garlic powder

¼ teaspoon sea salt

1. In your slow cooker, combine the beans, olive oil, cumin, garlic powder, and salt.

2. Add enough water to cover the beans by 2 inches.

3. Cover and cook on low until the beans are soft, 8 to 10 hours.

PER SERVING (½ CUP) Calories: 140; Total Fat: 2g; Saturated Fat: 0g; Cholesterol: 0mg; Carbohydrates: 22g; Fiber: 10g; Protein: 10g; Sodium: 56mg; Potassium: 407mg

Curried Lentils

SERVES 6 • **PREP TIME:** 10 MINUTES • **COOK TIME:** 8 HOURS
Super Quick Prep

Lentils and curry are a wonderful flavor combination. Lentils soak up the flavors of all the spices they are cooked with. You can use any color of lentils in this dish, such as red, brown, or green. Soak the lentils in water overnight to remove some of the compounds that contribute to the gassiness that often accompanies eating legumes.

2½ cups dried lentils, soaked overnight and rinsed

2 onions, chopped

1 tablespoon grated fresh ginger

4 cups Vegetable Broth (page 28), or store bought

½ cup canned light coconut milk

2 tablespoons curry powder

1 teaspoon garlic powder

1 teaspoon ground turmeric

¼ teaspoon sea salt

3 cups cooked Brown Rice (page 31)

1. In your slow cooker, combine the lentils, onions, ginger, broth, coconut milk, curry powder, garlic powder, turmeric, and salt.

2. Cover and cook on low for 8 hours.

3. Serve spooned over the cooked rice.

A BALANCED MEAL Add chopped carrots to the recipe before cooking, and stir in fresh spinach about 30 minutes before serving to make this a well-balanced dinner.

PER SERVING Calories: 538; Total Fat: 7g; Saturated Fat: 5g; Cholesterol: 0mg; Carbohydrates: 94g; Fiber: 28g; Protein: 26g; Sodium: 91mg; Potassium: 1056mg

Italian Spiced Lentils

SERVES 6 • **PREP TIME:** 10 MINUTES • **COOK TIME:** 8 HOURS
Super Quick Prep

Lentils make a great vegan protein source in Italian tomato sauce. Here, you spoon this fragrant sauce over cooked whole-wheat spaghetti, or the pasta of your choice, to make a protein-packed marinara sauce that's both easy and tasty. If you like, just before serving the sauce, stir in ¼ cup chopped fresh basil to add freshness to your pasta sauce.

1 pound dry lentils, soaked overnight and rinsed

1 onion, chopped

2 carrots, peeled and finely chopped

1 fennel bulb, finely chopped

2 (14-ounce) cans diced tomatoes, drained

5 cups Vegetable Broth (page 28), or store bought

2 teaspoons garlic powder

2 teaspoons dried Italian seasoning

½ teaspoon sea salt

3 cups cooked whole-wheat spaghetti

1. In your slow cooker, combine the lentils, onion, carrots, fennel, tomatoes, broth, garlic powder, Italian seasoning, and salt.

2. Cover and cook on low for 8 hours.

3. Serve spooned over the whole-wheat spaghetti.

PER SERVING Calories: 426; Total Fat: 2g; Saturated Fat: 0g; Cholesterol: 1mg; Carbohydrates: 80g; Fiber: 30g; Protein: 26g; Sodium: 223mg; Potassium: 1427mg

A BALANCED MEAL Serve with a simple romaine lettuce and tomato salad tossed with vinaigrette. To make the vinaigrette, whisk together ¾ cup olive oil, ¼ cup red wine vinegar, 1 tablespoon Dijon mustard, chopped fresh herbs of your choice, and a pinch of sea salt.

Red Lentil & Spinach Napa Rolls

SERVES 6 • **PREP TIME:** 10 MINUTES • **COOK TIME:** 8 HOURS
Super Quick Prep

The spiced lentil filling for these rolls simmers in the slow cooker all day, and then you just need to stir in chopped spinach and wrap the filling in tender napa cabbage leaves. This ups the veggie content while being absolutely delicious. It's also a great meal on the go. You can refrigerate the filling, tightly sealed, for up to 4 days.

1½ cups dried red lentils, soaked overnight and rinsed

1 onion, chopped

6 garlic cloves, minced

4 cups Vegetable Broth (page 28), or store bought

1 teaspoon ground cumin

½ teaspoon ground coriander

½ teaspoon curry powder

¼ teaspoon sea salt

2 cups chopped baby spinach

1 large head napa cabbage, separated into leaves

1. In your slow cooker, combine the lentils, onion, garlic, broth, cumin, coriander, curry powder, and salt.

2. Cover and cook on low for 8 hours.

3. Using a potato masher, mash the lentils. Stir in the baby spinach.

4. Serve with the napa cabbage leaves for wrapping.

PER SERVING Calories: 202; Total Fat: 1g; Saturated Fat: 0g; Cholesterol: 0mg; Carbohydrates: 37g; Fiber: 17g; Protein: 14g; Sodium: 108mg; Potassium: 721mg

Mushroom Risotto

SERVES 6 • **PREP TIME:** 10 MINUTES • **COOK TIME:** 8 HOURS

Traditional risotto is made with Arborio rice, a medium-grain white rice. However, in this dish, brown rice is used to increase the fiber content. You can find dried porcini mushrooms online or in the produce section of your local grocery store. Soak the dried mushrooms in the vegetable broth overnight for an intense mushroom flavor. If you can't find dried porcini mushrooms, use any variety of dried mushroom you can find.

2 ounces dried porcini mushrooms

4 cups Vegetable Broth (page 28), or store bought

1½ cups uncooked brown rice

1 onion, minced

1 pound fresh mushrooms, chopped

¼ cup dry white wine

1 teaspoon dried thyme

¼ teaspoon sea salt

¼ teaspoon freshly ground black pepper

4 ounces Neufchâtel cheese, cut into pieces

1. The night before cooking, put the dried porcini mushrooms in a small bowl, cover with the broth, and let soak overnight in the refrigerator.

2. The next day, remove the porcini mushrooms from the broth and roughly chop them. Add them, along with the broth, to the slow cooker.

3. Add the rice, onion, fresh mushrooms, white wine, thyme, salt, and pepper.

4. Cover and cook on low for 8 hours.

5. Stir in the Neufchâtel cheese just until it melts.

A BALANCED MEAL Stir in 2 cups cooked peas just before serving, to add some green to your risotto.

PER SERVING Calories: 299; Total Fat: 6g; Saturated Fat: 3g; Cholesterol: 14mg; Carbohydrates: 49g; Fiber: 5g; Protein: 11g; Sodium: 141mg; Potassium: 366mg

Cabbage Rolls

SERVES 6 • **PREP TIME:** 15 MINUTES • **COOK TIME:** 8 HOURS

Napa cabbage is pliable and easier to work with than other types of cabbage, so it's perfect for these cabbage rolls. However, if you are unable to find napa cabbage, feel free to use any type of green cabbage and blanch according to the directions in the Precooking Tip. These rolls keep well, so freeze any leftovers in single-serving containers for meals on the go.

For the sauce

3 (14-ounce) cans crushed tomatoes

1 onion, finely chopped

3 garlic cloves, minced

1 tablespoon low-sodium Worcestershire sauce

½ teaspoon sea salt

For the cabbage rolls

Nonstick cooking spray

3 cups cooked Brown Rice (page 31)

1 pound fresh mushrooms, finely chopped

1 onion, finely chopped

3 garlic cloves, minced

1 egg, beaten

1 tablespoon low-sodium Worcestershire sauce

1 teaspoon dried thyme

½ teaspoon sea salt

1 large head napa cabbage, separated into leaves

To make the sauce

In a large bowl, combine the tomatoes, onion, garlic, Worcestershire sauce, and salt, mixing well to form a sauce. Set aside.

To make the cabbage rolls

1. Spray the crock of your slow cooker with nonstick cooking spray.

2. In another bowl, mix together the cooked rice, mushrooms, onion, garlic, egg, Worcestershire sauce, thyme, and salt. »

PRECOOKING TIP To make the cabbage easier to work with, blanch the separated leaves in boiling water for 1 minute.

3. Scoop up some rice mixture in a ¼-cup measure, and drop it in the center of a cabbage leaf. Roll the cabbage leaf around the filling, making sure all the edges are tucked in. Repeat until you have used up all the filling.

4. Place the cabbage rolls in layers in the slow cooker, covering each layer with tomato sauce.

5. Cover and cook on low for 8 hours.

PER SERVING Calories: 309; Total Fat: 2g; Saturated Fat: 0g; Cholesterol: 27mg; Carbohydrates: 62g; Fiber: 11g; Protein: 13g; Sodium: 783mg; Potassium: 603mg

Rice & Kidney Bean Taco Salad

SERVES 4 • **PREP TIME:** 5 MINUTES • **COOK TIME:** 8 HOURS
Super Quick Prep

This easy taco topping transforms a bowl of salad into a savory meal. All you need to do at dinnertime is chop a few tomatoes and shred some romaine lettuce. Feel free to add any vegetables you like to your taco salad, such as diced avocado, cooked corn, scallions, or chopped cilantro. You can easily customize this salad according to what you like and what you have in the refrigerator.

1 cup uncooked brown rice

2 cups dried kidney beans, soaked overnight and rinsed

2 onions, chopped

1 (4-ounce) can diced jalapeño peppers, drained

8 cups Vegetable Broth (page 28), or store bought

1 tablespoon chili powder

1 teaspoon garlic powder

½ teaspoon sea salt

2 tomatoes, chopped

9 cups romaine lettuce, shredded

1. In your slow cooker, combine the rice, kidney beans, onion, jalapeños, broth, chili powder, garlic powder, and salt.

2. Cover and cook on low for 8 hours. Remove the lid and let cool for about 30 minutes.

3. In a large bowl, toss the tomatoes and romaine lettuce.

4. Add the cooked beans and rice. Toss to mix.

A BALANCED MEAL Top the salad with 1 cup shredded low-fat Cheddar cheese and 1 diced avocado to add protein and more vegetables to this dish.

PER SERVING Calories: 408; Total Fat: 2g; Saturated Fat: 0g; Cholesterol: 0mg; Carbohydrates: 80g; Fiber: 18g; Protein: 23g; Sodium: 516mg; Potassium: 1342mg

Red Beans & Rice

SERVES 6 • **PREP TIME:** 10 MINUTES • **COOK TIME:** 8 HOURS
Super Quick Prep

Red beans and rice is a Cajun favorite, redolent of smoky spice. To get the smoke flavor in your red beans and rice without using smoked meat, you add smoked paprika. Find a Creole seasoning blend in the spice aisle of your supermarket—many companies make them. They vary, but a typical blend includes onion and garlic powder, black and white pepper, oregano, thyme, basil, cayenne pepper, and sweet paprika.

1 pound dried red beans, soaked overnight and rinsed

2 green bell peppers, seeded and chopped

2 jalapeño peppers, seeded and chopped

8 cups Vegetable Broth (page 28), or store bought

1 tablespoon smoked paprika

1 tablespoon Creole seasoning

2 teaspoons garlic powder

1 teaspoon dried thyme

½ teaspoon sea salt

3 cups cooked Brown Rice (page 31)

1. In your slow cooker, combine the beans, bell peppers, jalapeños, broth, paprika, Creole seasoning, garlic powder, thyme, and salt.

2. Cover and cook on low for 8 hours.

3. Stir in the rice.

PER SERVING Calories: 467; Total Fat: 2g; Saturated Fat: 0g; Cholesterol: 0mg; Carbohydrates: 93g; Fiber: 15g; Protein: 22g; Sodium: 832mg; Potassium: 1391mg

Barley & Black Beans

SERVES 6 • **PREP TIME:** 10 MINUTES • **COOK TIME:** 8 HOURS
Super Quick Prep

Barley and black beans combine to make a complete protein—one that contains all nine of the essential amino acids we can't make ourselves. If you'd like, garnish this tasty Southwestern stew with your favorite condiments, such as a dollop of fat-free sour cream, chopped fresh cilantro, shredded low-fat Cheddar cheese, or chopped tomatoes.

1 cup uncooked pearl barley

2 cups dried black beans, soaked overnight and rinsed

1 onion, chopped

1 (14-ounce) can diced tomatoes and green chiles, drained

8 cups Vegetable Broth (page 28), or store bought

1 teaspoon garlic powder

1 teaspoon ground cumin

1 teaspoon chili powder

½ teaspoon sea salt

1 avocado, peeled, seeded, and cubed

1. In your slow cooker, combine the barley, black beans, onion, tomatoes, broth, garlic powder, cumin, chili powder, and salt.

2. Cover and cook on low for 8 hours.

3. Garnish with the cubed avocado.

PER SERVING Calories: 438; Total Fat: 8g; Saturated Fat: 2g; Cholesterol: 0mg; Carbohydrates: 81g; Fiber: 19g; Protein: 19g; Sodium: 173mg; Potassium: 1532mg

LEFTOVERS TIP You can make a tasty soup with the leftovers. Warm the leftovers on the stove top with 2 cups beef broth, and purée in the blender to serve.

Mexican Quinoa

SERVES 6 • **PREP TIME:** 10 MINUTES • **COOK TIME:** 8 HOURS
Super Quick Prep

Quinoa is a grain that originated in the Andean region of South America. It's high in protein, fiber, and B vitamins. This bright, attractive dish uses a mix of bell peppers and corn for color, along with canned tomatoes and peppers and jalapeños for heat. It freezes well and reheats easily, so it's an excellent meal to make ahead and freeze.

2 cups uncooked quinoa

2 cups cooked black beans (page 34), rinsed

1 green bell pepper, seeded and chopped

1 red bell pepper, seeded and chopped

2 jalapeño peppers, seeded and chopped

2 cups fresh or frozen corn

1 (14-ounce) can diced tomatoes and peppers, drained

4 cups Vegetable Broth (page 28), or store bought

1 teaspoon ground cumin

¼ cup chopped fresh cilantro

1. Rinse the quinoa in a fine-mesh sieve under running water.
2. In your slow cooker, combine the quinoa, black beans, jalapeños, corn, bell peppers, tomatoes and peppers, broth, and cumin.
3. Cover and cook on low for 8 hours.
4. Stir in the cilantro just before serving.

A BALANCED MEAL Add some low-fat dairy by topping the dish with a dollop of fat-free sour cream and 2 tablespoons grated low-fat Cheddar cheese.

PER SERVING Calories: 361; Total Fat: 5g; Saturated Fat: 1g; Cholesterol: 0mg; Carbohydrates: 67g; Fiber: 11g; Protein: 15g; Sodium: 135mg; Potassium: 1662mg

Quinoa-Stuffed Peppers

SERVES 6 • **PREP TIME:** 15 MINUTES • **COOK TIME:** 8 HOURS

Quinoa makes an excellent high-protein base for stuffed peppers. You can use any color of sweet bell pepper—red, orange, yellow, or green—or mix it up and use several different colors. The steam in the bottom of the slow cooker will plump up the quinoa, making it soft and tasty. Black beans combine with the quinoa to give you extra protein, so these peppers are a balanced meal all by themselves.

1 cup uncooked quinoa

3 cups cooked black beans (page 34), rinsed

1 (14-ounce) can diced tomatoes and peppers, drained

4 ounces shredded low-fat Cheddar cheese

1 teaspoon ground cumin

1 teaspoon garlic powder

¼ teaspoon sea salt

6 bell peppers, tops cut off, seeds and ribs carefully removed

1 cup Vegetable Broth (page 28), or store bought

¼ cup chopped fresh cilantro

1. Rinse the quinoa in a fine-mesh sieve under running water.

2. In a medium bowl, mix the quinoa, black beans, tomatoes and peppers, cheese, cumin, garlic powder, and salt.

3. Carefully stuff the peppers with the quinoa mixture.

4. Place the stuffed peppers in the slow cooker, cut-side up. Carefully pour the broth around the peppers.

5. Cover and cook on low for 8 hours.

6. Serve topped with the chopped cilantro.

PRECOOKING TIP For a slightly better texture, mash half of the black beans with a potato masher or process them in the food processor before mixing with the quinoa.

PER SERVING Calories: 345; Total Fat: 10g; Saturated Fat: 4g; Cholesterol: 20mg; Carbohydrates: 47g; Fiber: 11g; Protein: 18g; Sodium: 208mg; Potassium: 1317mg

Mediterranean Chickpeas & Quinoa

SERVES 6 • **PREP TIME:** 10 MINUTES • **COOK TIME:** 9 HOURS
Super Quick Prep

Lemon, garlic, and herbs make these chickpeas fragrant with Mediterranean spices. Chickpeas take a bit longer to cook than other dried legumes, so be sure to allow 9 hours to completely cook them. You can also use canned low-sodium chickpeas if you'd like this to cook more quickly, and reduce the cooking time to 8 hours. Make the quinoa ahead of time, and then reheat it just before serving.

1 pound dried chickpeas, soaked overnight and drained

1 onion, chopped

7 cups Vegetable Broth (page 28), or store bought

Zest and juice of 1 lemon

2 teaspoons garlic powder

1 tablespoon dried rosemary

1 teaspoon dried thyme

½ teaspoon sea salt

Pinch cayenne pepper

3 cups cooked Quinoa (page 32)

1. In your slow cooker, combine the chickpeas, onion, broth, lemon zest (reserve the juice), garlic powder, rosemary, thyme, salt, and cayenne.

2. Cover and cook on low for 9 hours.

3. Stir in the lemon juice. Serve spooned over the quinoa.

A BALANCED MEAL To add dairy and vegetables, garnish each serving with ¼ cup fat-free plain yogurt and some chopped cucumber.

PER SERVING Calories: 462; Total Fat: 7g; Saturated Fat: 1g; Cholesterol: 0mg; Carbohydrates: 81g; Fiber: 17g; Protein: 21g; Sodium: 191mg; Potassium: 1087mg

Whole-Wheat Pasta with Marinara Sauce

SERVES 6 • **PREP TIME:** 15 MINUTES • **COOK TIME:** 8 HOURS

This marinara sauce is loaded with flavorful vegetables and herbs. While in this recipe you use it to top whole-wheat pasta, you can also spoon it over quinoa, rice, or other grains, as well as (if you are not a vegetarian) cooked fish or poultry. It keeps well in the freezer for up to 1 year.

2 onions, chopped

5 bell peppers (any colors), seeded and chopped

3 large carrots, peeled and chopped

2 medium zucchini, chopped

2 (14-ounce) cans crushed tomatoes

¼ cup dry red wine

2 tablespoons Italian seasoning

2 teaspoons garlic powder

¼ teaspoon red pepper flakes

Pinch sea salt

3 cups cooked whole-wheat pasta

1. In your slow cooker, combine the onions, bell peppers, carrots, zucchini, crushed tomatoes, wine, Italian seasoning, garlic powder, red pepper flakes, and salt.

2. Cover and cook on low for 8 hours.

3. Serve over the cooked pasta.

PER SERVING Calories: 254; Total Fat: 3g; Saturated Fat: 0g; Cholesterol: 3mg; Carbohydrates: 48g; Fiber: 11g; Protein: 9g; Sodium: 336mg; Potassium: 598mg

Vegetable Lasagna

SERVES 6 • **PREP TIME:** 15 MINUTES • **COOK TIME:** 8 HOURS

It's easy to make a layered vegetable lasagna in your slow cooker. Make the marinara sauce from Whole-Wheat Pasta with Marinara Sauce (page 89) ahead of time, then use it for this lasagna. Don't forget to spray the sides and bottom of your slow cooker with nonstick cooking spray, which will make the lasagna lift out cleanly when it's time to serve.

Nonstick cooking spray

4 cups baby spinach

Leaves from 2 bunches fresh basil

2 teaspoons garlic powder

½ teaspoon sea salt

1½ cups skim ricotta cheese

10 cooked whole-wheat lasagna noodles

6 cups Marinara Sauce (page 89)

1 cup grated low-fat mozzarella cheese

1. Spray the crock of your slow cooker with nonstick cooking spray.

2. In a food processor, combine the spinach, basil, garlic powder, and salt. Pulse for 10 one-second pulses, until it resembles a pesto. You can also do this in a blender, or just very finely chop the spinach and basil with a knife and then mix it with the garlic powder and salt.

3. In a medium bowl, fold the spinach pesto mixture into the ricotta cheese.

4. Spread a thin layer of marinara sauce in the bottom of the slow cooker.

5. Add a layer of noodles. Spread the noodles with a thin layer of the ricotta mixture.

6. Cover with another layer of noodles. Spread on another layer of marinara.

7. Repeat steps 5 and 6 until you've used all your ingredients.

8. Top with the mozzarella.

9. Cover and cook on low for 8 hours.

PER SERVING Calories: 465; Total Fat: 15g; Saturated Fat: 7g; Cholesterol: 38mg; Carbohydrates: 57g; Fiber: 10g; Protein: 24g; Sodium: 374mg; Potassium: 661mg

Mushroom Stroganoff

SERVES 6 • **PREP TIME:** 10 MINUTES • **COOK TIME:** 8 HOURS
Super Quick Prep

Stroganoff is a Russian dish that traditionally uses beef. Here, meaty portobello mushrooms substitute for the chunks of beef, giving the dish an earthy and satisfying flavor. While the traditional recipe suggests serving it over egg noodles, you can also use whole-wheat pasta, brown rice, or quinoa. Be sure to use a spoon to scrape away the mushroom gills before you add them to the slow cooker.

2 pounds fresh portobello mushrooms, gills and stems removed, caps cut into ½-inch-thick slices

1 pound frozen pearl onions

1 teaspoon garlic powder

1½ cups Vegetable Broth (page 28), or store bought

¼ cup dry white wine

1 tablespoon low-sodium Worcestershire sauce

1 tablespoon Dijon mustard

2 cups fat-free sour cream

3 cups cooked whole-wheat egg noodles

1. In the slow cooker, combine the mushrooms, pearl onions, and garlic powder.

2. In a medium bowl, whisk together the broth, wine, Worcestershire sauce, and mustard. Add to the slow cooker.

3. Cover and cook on low for 8 hours.

4. Stir in the sour cream and serve over the egg noodles.

A BALANCED MEAL Sautéed asparagus makes an excellent accompaniment to the Stroganoff. You can either add 1-inch pieces of asparagus to the Stroganoff at the start of cooking, or sauté them in 1 tablespoon olive oil and serve them on the side.

PER SERVING Calories: 353; Total Fat: 2g; Saturated Fat: 1g; Cholesterol: 38mg; Carbohydrates: 63g; Fiber: 7g; Protein: 17g; Sodium: 137mg; Potassium: 868mg

Zucchini & Mushroom Casserole

SERVES 6 • **PREP TIME:** 15 MINUTES • **COOK TIME:** 8 HOURS

This simple egg casserole is really easy to make overnight in a slow cooker, so you have a hearty breakfast waiting for you when you get out of bed in the morning. It also makes a tasty lunch or supper, and it keeps well in the freezer, so you can make breakfast on the go for at least 4 days. The recipe calls for shiitake mushrooms, but you can substitute any type of sliced mushrooms you enjoy.

Nonstick cooking spray

8 ounces fresh shiitake
   mushrooms, sliced

1 onion, chopped

3 cups chopped baby spinach

1 zucchini, chopped

4 eggs

6 egg whites

¼ cup fat-free milk

1 tablespoon Dijon mustard

¼ teaspoon sea salt

¼ teaspoon freshly ground
   black pepper

½ cup grated low-fat
   Swiss cheese

1. Spray the crock of your slow cooker with nonstick cooking spray.

2. In a large bowl, toss together the mushrooms, onion, spinach, and zucchini.

3. In a medium bowl, whisk together the eggs, egg whites, milk, mustard, salt, and pepper.

4. Pour the egg mixture over the vegetables. Fold to combine.

5. Fold in the cheese.

6. Transfer the mixture to the slow cooker. Cover and cook on low for 8 hours.

7. Cut into wedges to serve.

PRECOOKING TIP Sauté the mushrooms, onion, spinach, and zucchini in 2 tablespoons olive oil until soft, about 5 minutes. Allow the vegetables to cool completely before adding the eggs.

PER SERVING Calories: 131; Total Fat: 5g; Saturated Fat: 2g; Cholesterol: 116mg; Carbohydrates: 10g; Fiber: 2g; Protein: 12g; Sodium: 312mg; Potassium: 361mg

White Bean & Rosemary Casserole

SERVES 6 • **PREP TIME:** 10 MINUTES • **COOK TIME:** 8 HOURS
Super Quick Prep

White beans and rosemary, punched up with a little garlic, are a classic and delicious flavor combination. There are as many ways to cook them—and as many ingredients to add—as there are cooks. Here a touch of citrusy orange zest adds a bright note. This makes a delicious entrée or serves as a tasty side dish. Spinach adds a touch of green and lots of nutrition.

2 cups dried white beans, soaked overnight and rinsed

1 onion, finely chopped

Zest of 1 orange

6 cups Vegetable Broth (page 28), or store bought

1 tablespoon dried rosemary

2 teaspoons garlic powder

½ teaspoon sea salt

¼ teaspoon freshly ground black pepper

4 cups baby spinach

1. In a slow cooker, combine the beans, onion, orange zest, broth, rosemary, garlic powder, salt, and pepper.

2. Cover and cook on low for 8 hours.

3. About 30 minutes before serving, stir in the spinach.

A BALANCED MEAL Spoon each serving over ½ cup cooked Quinoa (page 32) or cooked whole-wheat pasta to add some whole grains to your meal.

PER SERVING Calories: 256; Total Fat: 1g; Saturated Fat: 0g; Cholesterol: 0mg; Carbohydrates: 49g; Fiber: 11g; Protein: 17g; Sodium: 198mg; Potassium: 1567mg

Buffalo Cauliflower and Navy Beans

SERVES 2 • **PREP TIME:** 5 MINUTES • **COOK TIME:** 8 HOURS
Super Quick Prep

"Buffalo," once a term used only for spicy fried chicken wings, now encompasses a variety of spicy, savory dishes, including this quick and easy vegan chili. Cook the navy beans ahead of time, and then just toss them into the slow cooker with the other ingredients. The most commonly used Louisiana hot sauce for buffalo flavoring is Frank's RedHot, but any Louisiana hot sauce will do. The result is a spicy chili that's perfect for a game-day meal.

1 head cauliflower, cut into small florets

1 red onion, finely chopped

2 celery stalks, diced

3 cups cooked navy beans (page 34), rinsed

½ cup Poultry Broth (page 29), or store bought

½ cup Louisiana hot sauce

1 tablespoon chili powder

2 teaspoons ground cumin

½ teaspoon sea salt

Pinch cayenne pepper

¼ cup crumbled blue cheese

1. In your slow cooker, combine the cauliflower, onion, celery, navy beans, broth, hot sauce, chili powder, cumin, salt, and cayenne.

2. Cover and cook on low for 8 hours.

3. Serve garnished with the blue cheese.

PER SERVING Calories: 190; Total Fat: 3g; Saturated Fat: 1g; Cholesterol: 4mg; Carbohydrates: 33g; Fiber: 13g; Protein: 11g; Sodium: 293mg; Potassium: 2605mg

Chinese Hot Pot

SERVES 6 • **PREP TIME:** 15 MINUTES • **COOK TIME:** 8 HOURS

Hot pot is a traditional Asian dish in which vegetables are cooked in simmering broth, sometimes right at the table, other times in advance in a casserole. This one has a traditional Asian flavor profile, and using a slow cooker is the perfect way to simmer the vegetables in broth. Garlic, ginger, and sesame oil add traditional Asian flavors.

1 pound fresh shiitake
mushrooms, sliced

2 cups snow peas

8 scallions, sliced

2 tablespoons grated
fresh ginger

8 cups Vegetable Broth
(page 28), or store bought

1 tablespoon low-sodium
soy sauce

1 teaspoon garlic powder

½ teaspoon sea salt

1 tablespoon sesame-chili oil

¼ cup chopped fresh cilantro

1. In your slow cooker, combine the mushrooms, snow peas, scallions, ginger, broth, soy sauce, garlic powder, and salt.

2. Cover and cook on low for 8 hours.

3. Just before serving, stir in the sesame-chili oil and cilantro.

A BALANCED MEAL Serve spooned over ½ cup cooked brown rice per person to add grains to this meal.

PER SERVING Calories: 104; Total Fat: 1g; Saturated Fat: 0g; Cholesterol: 0mg; Carbohydrates: 24g; Fiber: 4g; Protein: 4g; Sodium: 490mg; Potassium: 418mg

Barley, Mushrooms & Carrots

SERVES 6 • **PREP TIME:** 10 MINUTES • **COOK TIME:** 8 HOURS
Super Quick Prep

Barley and mushrooms make a tasty combo that really sticks to your ribs. Barley is hearty and flavorful, while mushrooms bring a meaty, earthy flavor profile to this simple yet satisfying dish.

2 cups pearl barley

5 cups Vegetable Broth (page 28), or store bought

3 large carrots, peeled and chopped

8 ounces shiitake mushrooms, sliced

1 onion, peeled and chopped

½ teaspoon salt

1 teaspoon dried rosemary

⅛ teaspoon black pepper

1 cup fresh or frozen peas

1. In your slow cooker, combine the barley, broth, carrots, mushrooms, onion, salt, rosemary, and pepper.

2. Cover and cook on low for 7½ hours.

3. Stir in the peas. Cover and cook for an additional 30 minutes.

PER SERVING (1 Cup) Calories: 351; Total Fat: 2g; Saturated Fat: 1g; Cholesterol: 0mg; Carbohydrates: 72g; Fiber 15g; Protein: 14g; Sodium: 324mg; Potassium: 548mg

Poultry & Seafood

Turkey, Sausage & Egg Breakfast Casserole

SERVES 6 • **PREP TIME:** 15 MINUTES • **COOK TIME:** 8 HOURS

This is a great recipe for when you want a hearty breakfast but there just isn't enough time in the morning to cook it. Mix this up before you go to bed the night before, then set your slow cooker on low to cook it throughout the night. In the morning, you'll awaken to the delicious aroma of a breakfast that will start your day off right.

Nonstick cooking spray

12 ounces cooked turkey breakfast sausage

2 red bell peppers, seeded and chopped

1 onion, chopped

8 ounces fresh mushrooms, chopped

6 eggs

6 egg whites

½ cup skim milk

¼ teaspoon freshly ground black pepper

¼ cup low-fat grated Parmesan cheese

1. Spray the crock of your slow cooker with nonstick cooking spray.

2. In a large bowl, combine the cooked sausage, bell pepper, onion, and mushrooms.

3. In a medium bowl, whisk together the eggs, egg whites, milk, and pepper.

4. Pour the eggs over the sausage mixture and mix well.

5. Fold in the cheese.

6. Pour the mixture into the slow cooker. Cook on low for 8 hours.

7. Cut into wedges to serve.

PRECOOKING TIP Brown the sausage, onion, pepper, and mushrooms in 2 tablespoons olive oil before adding to the eggs. Allow to cool completely before adding the eggs and cheese.

PER SERVING Calories: 237; Total Fat: 14g; Saturated Fat: 4g; Cholesterol: 218mg; Carbohydrates: 7g; Fiber: 2g; Protein: 23g; Sodium: 579mg; Potassium: 543mg

Asian Turkey Lettuce Wraps

SERVES 6 • **PREP TIME:** 10 MINUTES • **COOK TIME:** 8 HOURS
Super Quick Prep

These turkey lettuce wraps taste like the filling of pot stickers, with a classic Asian profile of ginger, garlic, and cilantro. You can dip the wraps in the optional sweet and sour lime dip, which adds even more fantastic flavors to this tasty dish.

For the wraps

1 pound ground turkey breast

1 pound fresh shiitake
   mushrooms, sliced

6 scallions, chopped

1 teaspoon grated fresh ginger

½ cup Poultry Broth (page 29),
   or store bought

1 tablespoon low-sodium
   soy sauce

1 teaspoon Sriracha sauce

1 teaspoon garlic powder

¼ cup chopped fresh cilantro

12 large butter lettuce leaves

**For the optional
dipping sauce**

Juice of 2 limes

Zest of 1 lime

2 tablespoons rice vinegar

1 tablespoon honey

½ teaspoon Sriracha sauce

Pinch sea salt

To make the wraps

1. Crumble the ground turkey into your slow cooker.

2. Add the mushrooms, scallions, ginger, broth, soy sauce, Sriracha, and garlic powder.

3. Cover and cook on low for 8 hours.

4. Stir in the cilantro.

5. Serve wrapped in lettuce leaves, alongside the sauce for dipping, if desired.

To make the dipping sauce

In a small bowl, whisk together all the ingredients.

PER SERVING (INCLUDES DIPPING SAUCE) Calories: 220; Total Fat: 7g; Saturated Fat: 2g; Cholesterol: 57mg; Carbohydrates: 16g; Fiber: 2g; Protein: 24g; Sodium: 462mg; Potassium: 407mg

Turkey & Wild Rice

SERVES 6 • **PREP TIME:** 10 MINUTES • **COOK TIME:** 8 HOURS
Super Quick Prep

Turkey thighs, fresh cranberries, and wild rice combine to make a delicious slow cooker dish you're sure to love. Wild rice isn't actually related to rice. Instead, it's harvested from four different species of water grasses, but its rice-like texture and shape give it its name. Nutritionally, wild rice is a whole grain, full of healthy fiber.

1 pound boneless, skinless turkey thighs, cut into 1-inch chunks

1 cup uncooked wild rice

1 onion, chopped

1 cup fresh or frozen cranberries

Zest and juice of 1 orange

3 cups Poultry Broth (page 29), or store bought

1 teaspoon garlic powder

1 teaspoon dried thyme

½ teaspoon sea salt

¼ teaspoon freshly ground black pepper

1. In your slow cooker, combine the turkey, wild rice, onion, cranberries, orange zest (reserve the juice), broth, garlic powder, thyme, salt, and pepper.

2. Cover and cook on low for 8 hours.

3. Stir in the fresh orange juice before serving.

SMART SHOPPING TIP
Purchase bone-in, skin-on turkey thighs and remove the skin and bones yourself. This will save you money, because boneless, skinless turkey thighs cost more.

PER SERVING Calories: 202; Total Fat: 2g; Saturated Fat: 1g; Cholesterol: 63mg; Carbohydrates: 25g; Fiber: 3g; Protein: 21g; Sodium: 212mg; Potassium: 405mg

Stuffed Turkey Breast

SERVES 6 • **PREP TIME:** 15 MINUTES • **COOK TIME:** 8 HOURS

If you like the traditional Thanksgiving combination of turkey and stuffing, you'll enjoy this slow-cooker stuffed turkey breast. It replaces the traditional bread stuffing with quinoa for extra protein and fiber, but it retains all the flavor of the original with traditional spices like sage and thyme. This recipe uses a boneless, skin-on turkey breast. If your turkey breast comes with the bones in, just pry them out with a small, sharp knife before you start. Or you can cut into the breast meat, parallel to the ribs, to create a cavity, then push the stuffing into the cavity. The skin keeps the meat moist while cooking, then is removed before serving.

3 cups cooked Quinoa (page 32)

2 onions, finely chopped

2 carrots, peeled and finely chopped

2 celery stalks, finely chopped

1 egg, beaten

1 teaspoon dried thyme

1 teaspoon dried sage

1 teaspoon sea salt, divided

½ teaspoon freshly ground black pepper, divided

1 (2-pound) boneless, skin-on turkey breast

½ cup Poultry Broth (page 29), or store bought

1. In a medium bowl, combine the quinoa, onions, carrots, celery, egg, thyme, sage, ½ teaspoon of sea salt, and ¼ teaspoon of black pepper.

2. Put the turkey breast on a large cutting board, skin-side down, between two pieces of plastic wrap, and pound it slightly to flatten.

3. Spread the filling evenly over the flesh side of the breast.

4. Roll the breast around the filling, skin-side out. Sprinkle the skin side with the remaining ½ teaspoon of salt and ¼ teaspoon of black pepper.

5. Put the stuffed turkey breast into your slow cooker. Add the broth. Cover and cook for 8 hours on low.

6. Remove the turkey skin before slicing and serving.

PRECOOKING TIP For better flavor, sauté the onions, carrots, and celery in 2 tablespoons olive oil before mixing with the quinoa and herbs.

PER SERVING Calories: 361; Total Fat: 4g; Saturated Fat: 1g; Cholesterol: 121mg; Carbohydrates: 33g; Fiber: 5g; Protein: 45g; Sodium: 451mg; Potassium: 838mg

Spinach and Quinoa–Stuffed Chicken Breasts

SERVES 4 • **PREP TIME:** 15 MINUTES • **COOK TIME:** 8 HOURS

While this takes a little prep work, the result is worth it. Tarragon, mushrooms, and white wine are a classic French flavor combination that's fragrant, delicate, and delicious. If you can find it, use fresh tarragon. However, dried tarragon will work just fine if that's all you can find. Both have a savory herbal aroma reminiscent of licorice.

2 boneless, skinless chicken breasts, cut in half horizontally to make 4 cutlets total

1 teaspoon sea salt, divided

½ teaspoon freshly ground black pepper, divided

2 cups baby spinach, stems trimmed

2 cups cooked Quinoa (page 32)

½ onion, finely chopped

4 ounces fresh mushrooms, finely chopped

2 teaspoons dried tarragon or 1 teaspoon minced fresh tarragon

Zest of 1 lemon

1½ cups dry white wine

1. Place each chicken breast cutlet between 2 pieces of parchment paper or plastic wrap and pound them flat.

2. Sprinkle the chicken cutlets with ½ teaspoon of salt and ¼ teaspoon of pepper.

3. Arrange the spinach leaves in a layer on top of each seasoned cutlet.

4. In a small bowl, mix the quinoa, onion, mushrooms, tarragon, lemon zest, remaining ½ teaspoon of salt, and remaining ¼ teaspoon of pepper.

5. Spread the stuffing on top of the spinach on each cutlet.

6. Roll each chicken cutlet around the filling, tying with kitchen twine to keep them rolled.

PRECOOKING TIP Sauté the onion and mushrooms in 2 tablespoons olive oil before adding them to the quinoa. Once the chicken rolls have been assembled, sear them for 3 minutes on all sides before adding them to the slow cooker.

7. Place the stuffed chicken rolls in a single layer in the food processor. Add the wine.

8. Cover and cook on low for 8 hours.

9. Remove the chicken rolls from the slow cooker. Snip and remove the kitchen twine.

10. Transfer the wine and any accumulated juices to a small saucepan and simmer until it reduces by half, about 5 minutes. Spoon over the chicken.

PER SERVING Calories: 381; Total Fat: 8g; Saturated Fat: 2g; Cholesterol: 63mg; Carbohydrates: 33g; Fiber: 4g; Protein: 28g; Sodium: 386mg; Potassium: 526mg

Chicken Burrito Bowls

SERVES 6 • **PREP TIME:** 10 MINUTES • **COOK TIME:** 8 HOURS
Super Quick Prep

These "naked burritos" have all the tasty burrito filling without the outer shell. The best thing about these burrito bowls is they are completely customizable. Add any toppings you wish in addition to those suggested here, such as low-fat shredded cheese, chopped fresh cilantro, pico de gallo, or low-fat sour cream, to customize the burrito bowl to your taste.

1 pound boneless, skinless chicken breasts

Juice and zest of 1 lime

1 cup Poultry Broth (page 29), or store bought

1 teaspoon chili powder

1 teaspoon ground cumin

½ teaspoon sea salt

3 cups cooked Brown Rice (page 31)

6 scallions, chopped, for serving

3 tomatoes, chopped, for serving

1 avocado, peeled, pitted, and cubed, for serving

1. In your slow cooker, combine the chicken breasts, lime zest (reserve the juice), broth, chili powder, cumin, and salt.

2. Cover and cook on low for 8 hours.

3. Using two forks, shred the chicken breasts.

4. Divide the brown rice among 6 bowls. Add the shredded chicken on top of the rice, then top with the scallions, tomatoes, and avocado—or garnishes of your choice. Sprinkle with the reserved lime juice.

PER SERVING Calories: 405; Total Fat: 14g; Saturated Fat: 3g; Cholesterol: 67mg; Carbohydrates: 43g; Fiber: 5g; Protein: 27g; Sodium: 235mg; Potassium: 675mg

Maple-Soy Glazed Chicken Drumsticks

SERVES 6 • **PREP TIME:** 10 MINUTES • **COOK TIME:** 8 HOURS
Super Quick Prep

These sticky drumsticks are really easy to make and always a favorite with kids, who love the sweet and salty flavor. For a slightly more grown-up (spicy) version, add 1 tablespoon Sriracha sauce to the syrup glaze. You can also replace the maple syrup with honey (in that case, add the zest of an orange for a lovely citrus flavor). Be sure to use pure maple syrup, not the artificially flavored stuff.

12 chicken drumsticks

½ cup pure maple syrup

¼ cup low-sodium soy sauce

1 teaspoon grated
  fresh ginger

1 teaspoon cornstarch

½ teaspoon garlic powder

¼ teaspoon freshly ground
  black pepper

4 scallions, sliced

1 teaspoon sesame seeds

1. Put the drumsticks in your slow cooker.
2. In a small bowl, whisk together the maple syrup, soy sauce, ginger, cornstarch, garlic powder, and pepper.
3. Pour the sauce over the drumsticks and stir to coat.
4. Cover and cook on low for 8 hours.
5. Garnish with the scallions and sesame seeds before serving.

A BALANCED MEAL
Serve with cooked rice and steamed green beans for a well-balanced dinner.

PER SERVING Calories: 237; Total Fat: 6g; Saturated Fat: 1g; Cholesterol: 81mg; Carbohydrates: 20g; Fiber: 0g; Protein: 26g; Sodium: 665mg; Potassium: 274mg

Arroz con Pollo

SERVES 6 • **PREP TIME:** 10 MINUTES • **COOK TIME:** 8 HOURS
Super Quick Prep

Arroz con pollo simply means rice with chicken. It's a traditional Latin American and Spanish recipe with plenty of flavor—a second cousin of paella and pilaf. Feel free to adjust the heat to your taste by adding more or less cayenne pepper. The amount suggested here will add mild but not overpowering heat. If you wish, garnish with wedges of lime and chopped fresh cilantro.

6 bone-in, skin-on chicken thighs

2 onions, chopped

1 (14-ounce) can diced tomatoes and peppers, drained

1 cup uncooked brown rice

3 cups Poultry Broth (page 29), or store bought

1 teaspoon garlic powder

1 teaspoon ground cumin

1 teaspoon dried oregano

¼ teaspoon sea salt

⅛ teaspoon cayenne pepper

1. In your slow cooker, combine all the ingredients.
2. Cover and cook on low for 8 hours.
3. Remove the skin from the chicken before serving.

PRECOOKING TIP To develop better flavor, brown the chicken thighs in 2 tablespoons olive oil for about 5 minutes per side before adding them to the slow cooker.

PER SERVING Calories: 409; Total Fat: 25g; Saturated Fat: 5g; Cholesterol: 106mg; Carbohydrates: 31g; Fiber: 3g; Protein: 32g; Sodium: 205mg; Potassium: 651mg

Lime & Jalapeño Chicken Thighs

SERVES 4 • **PREP TIME:** 15 MINUTES • **COOK TIME:** 8 HOURS

If you like your chicken with a little bit of heat and a little bit of sweet, you'll enjoy these chicken thighs. They have a sweet, spicy, sticky glaze that's bursting with Latin American flavors. The acidity of the lime cuts nicely through the heat of the jalapeño. To control the heat in the jalapeños, remove the seeds and ribs. If you want a little more spice, leave them in—or toss in an extra pepper.

4 bone-in, skinless
  chicken thighs

¼ cup honey

Juice of 2 limes

Zest of 1 lime

1 jalapeño pepper, seeded
  and minced

½ teaspoon garlic powder

½ teaspoon sea salt

¼ cup chopped fresh cilantro

1. Put the chicken thighs in your slow cooker.
2. In a small bowl, whisk together the honey, lime juice, lime zest, jalapeño, garlic powder, and salt.
3. Pour the mixture over the chicken.
4. Cover and cook on low for 8 hours.
5. Garnish with the cilantro before serving.

A BALANCED MEAL Serve with brown rice and a tossed salad with a simple vinaigrette made from 3 tablespoons olive oil, 1 tablespoon freshly squeezed lime juice, ½ a minced jalapeño pepper, a drizzle of honey, and a pinch of salt.

PER SERVING Calories: 314; Total Fat: 16g; Saturated Fat: 5g; Cholesterol: 94mg; Carbohydrates: 18g; Fiber: 0g; Protein: 26g; Sodium: 277mg; Potassium: 359mg

Chicken Cacciatore

SERVES 6 • **PREP TIME:** 10 MINUTES • **COOK TIME:** 8 HOURS
Super Quick Prep

An Italian classic, chicken cacciatore is a delicious, hearty stew that translates to "chicken prepared hunter-style." That includes traditional Italian flavors such as garlic, tomatoes, mushrooms, and oregano. Traditional chicken cacciatore uses a whole chicken cut into pieces, but to save fat, this recipe uses skinless, boneless chicken thighs instead.

1 pound boneless, skinless chicken thighs, cut into 1-inch pieces

2 onions, sliced

1 pound fresh mushrooms, halved

2 green bell peppers, seeded and sliced

1 (14-ounce) can diced tomatoes, with their juice

1½ teaspoons garlic powder

1 teaspoon dried Italian seasoning

¼ teaspoon sea salt

¼ teaspoon freshly ground black pepper

¼ teaspoon red pepper flakes

1. Combine all the ingredients in your slow cooker.

2. Cover and cook on low for 8 hours.

3. Serve the chicken pieces with the sauce spooned over the top.

PER SERVING Calories: 204; Total Fat: 6g; Saturated Fat: 2g; Cholesterol: 68mg; Carbohydrates: 12g; Fiber: 3g; Protein: 26g; Sodium: 154mg; Potassium: 729mg

A BALANCED MEAL Serve the chicken and sauce over ½ cup (per serving) whole-wheat spaghetti to add whole grains, and add 2 tablespoons (per serving) low-fat Parmesan cheese for dairy.

Peach-Bourbon Chicken

SERVES 6 • **PREP TIME:** 15 MINUTES • **COOK TIME:** 8 HOURS

This sweet and boozy barbecue sauce seems sinfully delicious, but you can eat it without guilt. Simmering the chicken in the sauce makes it moist and flavorful, allowing the taste of the sauce to permeate the meat. The sauce has everything your palate wants: sweet, salt, smoke, and just a touch of heat.

6 boneless, skinless chicken thighs

1½ cups peeled and chopped fresh peaches

1 (14-ounce) can tomato sauce

½ cup bourbon

⅓ cup apple cider vinegar

¼ cup pure maple syrup

¾ teaspoon liquid smoke

1 teaspoon garlic powder

½ teaspoon sea salt

¼ teaspoon cayenne pepper

1. Put the chicken thighs in your slow cooker.

2. In a small saucepan, combine all the remaining ingredients.

3. Simmer over medium-low heat, stirring frequently and mashing the peaches with a spoon, until the sauce thickens, about 5 minutes.

4. Cool the sauce for 5 minutes. Pour it over the chicken.

5. Cover and cook on low for 8 hours.

PER SERVING Calories: 325; Total Fat: 9g; Saturated Fat: 2g; Cholesterol: 101mg; Carbohydrates: 16g; Fiber: 2g; Protein: 34g; Sodium: 625mg; Potassium: 665mg

A BALANCED MEAL Bake sweet potatoes to serve on the side and top them with fat-free sour cream. For a vegetable, make a simple slaw with shredded cabbage and a vinaigrette made from ¾ cup olive oil, ¼ cup apple cider vinegar, the juice and zest of 1 orange, 1 tablespoon Dijon mustard, 2 minced garlic cloves, and ¼ teaspoon sea salt.

Jambalaya

SERVES 6 • **PREP TIME:** 15 MINUTES • **COOK TIME:** 9 HOURS

Jambalaya is a classic Louisiana Creole dish of smoky sausage, chicken, and delectable shrimp in a spicy tomato broth served with hot rice. Creole means it has Spanish and French influences, and in fact, the word likely comes from a Provençal French word that means a mash-up, and can also refer to a pilaf. Cooking jambalaya in the slow cooker gives the flavors plenty of time to really blend together to develop a thick, rich, fragrant stew.

6 boneless, skinless chicken thighs, cut into 1-inch pieces

6 ounces smoked turkey sausage, cut into 1-inch pieces

2 cups chopped okra

2 green bell peppers, seeded and chopped

1 onion, chopped

6 garlic cloves, chopped

2 (14-ounce) cans diced tomatoes and peppers, with their juice

½ teaspoon sea salt

¼ teaspoon cayenne pepper

6 ounces raw shrimp, peeled and deveined

3 cups cooked Brown Rice (page 31)

1. In your slow cooker, combine the chicken, turkey sausage, okra, bell peppers, onion, garlic, tomatoes and peppers (with their juice), salt, and cayenne.

2. Cover and cook on low for 8 hours.

3. Stir in the shrimp. Cover and cook for 1 more hour.

4. Serve spooned over the cooked rice.

SMART SHOPPING TIP You can buy flash-frozen shrimp at the grocery store, which are cheaper than fresh shrimp. Add the shrimp to the slow cooker when they are still frozen.

PER SERVING Calories: 485; Total Fat: 11g; Saturated Fat: 3g; Cholesterol: 162mg; Carbohydrates: 49g; Fiber: 6g; Protein: 46g; Sodium: 154mg; Potassium: 729mg; Sodium: 571mg; Potassium: 1136mg

Shrimp & Peppers with Rice

SERVES 4 • **PREP TIME:** 10 MINUTES • **COOK TIME:** 8½ HOURS
Super Quick Prep

To keep the shrimp tender in this dish, add them (along with the peas) in the last 30 minutes of cooking and turn the slow cooker on high. As soon as the shrimp are pink, they're ready to eat. The rest of the stew simmers throughout the day, allowing the flavors to blend. Choose a variety of colors for the bell peppers, to make the dish look bright and festive.

6 bell peppers, various colors, seeded and sliced

1 onion, sliced

2 cups uncooked brown rice

3⅔ cups Vegetable Broth (page 28), or store bought

1 cup dry white wine

2 teaspoons garlic powder

¼ teaspoon sea salt

¼ teaspoon freshly ground black pepper

12 ounces fresh shrimp, peeled and deveined

1 cup fresh or frozen peas

1. In your slow cooker, combine the bell peppers, onion, rice, broth, wine, garlic powder, salt, and pepper.

2. Cover and cook on low for 8 hours.

3. Stir in the shrimp and peas. Turn the slow cooker to high.

4. Cover and cook just until the shrimp are pink, about 30 more minutes.

PER SERVING Calories: 611; Total Fat: 5g; Saturated Fat: 1g; Cholesterol: 179mg; Carbohydrates: 100g; Fiber: 10g; Protein: 31g; Sodium: 228mg; Potassium: 653mg

Cioppino

SERVES 6 • **PREP TIME:** 15 MINUTES • **COOK TIME:** 9 HOURS

Cioppino is a classic seafood stew developed by Italian immigrants in the seafood-rich city of San Francisco. Feel free to add any seafood you like to the stew—don't feel limited by what is suggested here. While you can add the fish in the morning to save time, the texture will be better if you wait until there's just an hour left of cooking.

2 onions, chopped

2 (14-ounce) cans
    tomato sauce

2 cups Vegetable Broth
    (page 28), or store bought

1 cup dry white wine

1 tablespoon dried
    Italian seasoning

2 teaspoons garlic powder

¼ teaspoon freshly ground
    black pepper

Pinch red pepper flakes

6 ounces raw shrimp,
    peeled and deveined

6 ounces cod, skinned and
    cut into ½-inch pieces

1. In your slow cooker, combine the onions, tomato sauce, broth, wine, Italian seasoning, garlic powder, black pepper, and red pepper flakes.

2. Cover and cook on low for 8 hours.

3. Stir in the shrimp and cod. Cover and continue to cook until the shrimp are pink and the fish is opaque, about 1 hour more.

A BALANCED MEAL Serve with ½ cup cooked whole-wheat pasta in each bowl and top with 2 tablespoons low-fat Parmesan cheese, to add grains and dairy.

PER SERVING Calories: 158; Total Fat: 2g; Saturated Fat: 0g; Cholesterol: 77mg; Carbohydrates: 15g; Fiber: 3g; Protein: 15g; Sodium: 789mg; Potassium: 661mg

Quinoa Seafood Stew

SERVES 6 • **PREP TIME:** 15 MINUTES • **COOK TIME:** 8½ HOURS

This stew has Spanish flavors of citrus and smoked paprika that make it fragrant and inviting. Feel free to add any type of seafood in any combination you like. Try using fresh calamari (squid), scallops, or other white fish in place of the halibut recommended here. Make the quinoa and sauce in the slow cooker, then add the seafood in the last 30 minutes of cooking, to keep its texture.

1 onion, sliced

3 carrots, peeled and sliced

1 cup uncooked quinoa

Juice and zest of 1 lemon

3 cups Vegetable Broth (page 28), or store bought

1 cup dry white wine

1 teaspoon smoked paprika

½ teaspoon ground turmeric

½ teaspoon sea salt

¼ teaspoon freshly ground black pepper

12 ounces halibut, skinned and cut into ½-inch pieces

1. In your slow cooker, combine the onion, carrots, quinoa, lemon zest (reserve the juice), broth, white wine, paprika, turmeric, salt, and pepper.

2. Cover and cook on low for 8 hours.

3. Stir in the halibut. Turn the slow cooker to high.

4. Cover and cook until the halibut is opaque, about 20 minutes.

5. Stir in the reserved lemon juice.

SMART SHOPPING TIP
Halibut can be a bit expensive, but you can replace it with a less expensive whitefish, such as cod.

PER SERVING Calories: 225; Total Fat: 3g; Saturated Fat: 0g; Cholesterol: 18mg; Carbohydrates: 27g; Fiber: 3g; Protein: 16g; Sodium: 226mg; Potassium: 475mg

Beef, Pork & Lamb

Shredded Beef Sandwiches

SERVES 6 • **PREP TIME:** 10 MINUTES • **COOK TIME:** 8 HOURS
Super Quick Prep

This peppery beef is the perfect filling for sandwiches. Cook it in the slow cooker all day, and then serve it on your favorite buns along with a side of coleslaw or a crisp green salad. It's also a great make-ahead that you can pack up in sealed containers and take for lunch, reheating it in the microwave if you wish. If you want to skip the bread, you can also use this as a tasty lettuce wrap filling.

1 pound pot roast, trimmed of visible fat

1 cup Beef Broth (page 30), or store bought

1 teaspoon onion powder

1 teaspoon garlic powder

1 teaspoon ground cumin

1 teaspoon freshly ground black pepper

¼ teaspoon sea salt

1 avocado, peeled, pitted, and mashed

6 whole-wheat sandwich rolls

1 tomato, chopped

1. Put the pot roast in your slow cooker. Add the broth, onion powder, garlic powder, cumin, pepper, and salt.

2. Cover and cook on low for 8 hours.

3. Remove the beef from the slow cooker and shred it with two forks. Return the meat to the slow cooker and toss to coat with the broth.

4. Spread some mashed avocado on the bottom half of each sandwich roll. Add the beef and top with the chopped tomato. Close the sandwiches and serve.

PER SERVING Calories: 367; Total Fat: 14g; Saturated Fat: 4g; Cholesterol: 68mg; Carbohydrates: 33g; Fiber: 7g; Protein: 30g; Sodium: 337mg; Potassium: 551mg

Sloppy Joes

SERVES 4 • **PREP TIME:** 15 MINUTES • **COOK TIME:** 8 HOURS

These sloppy Joes are served in lettuce cups, but if you prefer to have a sandwich, feel free to use a whole-wheat bun. The mixture of meat and vegetables is zesty, slightly sweet, and spicy, so it's a perfectly balanced bite. Serve it topped with a simple slaw for a tasty balanced meal.

1 pound extra-lean ground beef

2 onions, chopped

2 green bell peppers, seeded and chopped

1 (14-ounce) can crushed tomatoes

½ cup apple cider vinegar

2 tablespoons honey

Juice and zest of 1 orange

¼ teaspoon sea salt

¼ teaspoon cayenne pepper

4 large iceberg lettuce leaves

1. Crumble the ground beef into small pieces in your slow cooker.
2. Add the onions, bell peppers, tomatoes, vinegar, honey, orange juice and orange zest, salt, and cayenne.
3. Cover and cook on low for 8 hours.
4. Spoon the mixture into the lettuce leaves and serve.

PER SERVING Calories: 261; Total Fat: 5g; Saturated Fat: 2g; Cholesterol: 60mg; Carbohydrates: 26g; Fiber: 6g; Protein: 28g; Sodium: 390mg; Potassium: 713mg

A BALANCED MEAL Stir in 2 cups cooked Brown Rice (page 31) after cooking. Top with a simple slaw made of shredded cabbage with a vinaigrette made from ½ cup olive oil, the juice of 1 orange, 2 tablespoons apple cider vinegar, 1 tablespoon Dijon mustard, and a pinch each of sea salt and freshly ground black pepper.

Korean Barbecue Beef Sandwiches

SERVES 8 • **PREP TIME:** 10 MINUTES • **COOK TIME:** 8 HOURS
Super Quick Prep

These shredded beef sandwiches have a tasty Asian flavor profile reminiscent of Korean barbecue. Trim as much of the visible fat from the meat as possible, leaving some marbling to keep it tender. Then, shred the beef with forks, skim the excess fat from the broth, and return the beef to the sauce to make your sandwiches. The recipe calls for Sriracha, which is a spicy Asian chili sauce. You can find it in the Asian foods aisle at some supermarkets, Asian grocery stores, or online.

2 pounds boneless chuck roast, trimmed of excess fat

½ cup rice vinegar

¼ cup olive oil

2 tablespoons Sriracha sauce

2 tablespoons low-sodium soy sauce

2 tablespoons honey

½ teaspoon toasted sesame oil

2 tablespoons grated fresh ginger

2 teaspoons garlic powder

8 whole-wheat hamburger buns

1. Put the chuck roast whole in the slow cooker.
2. In a blender, blend the vinegar, olive oil, Sriracha, soy sauce, honey, sesame oil, ginger, and garlic powder until well mixed. Pour the mixture over the beef.
3. Cover and cook on low for 8 hours.
4. Transfer the roast to a cutting board and shred the meat with two forks. Skim the fat from the sauce and discard. Return the beef to the sauce and toss to coat. Serve on the buns.

A BALANCED MEAL The spicy, salty flavor of the beef needs some acid to balance it. A nice slaw made from julienned apples and jicama tossed with some rice vinegar, olive oil, and minced garlic is the perfect accompaniment.

PER SERVING Calories: 588; Total Fat: 38g; Saturated Fat: 12g; Cholesterol: 115mg; Carbohydrates: 25g; Fiber: 3g; Protein: 35g; Sodium: 590mg; Potassium: 353mg

Peppered Pulled Beef Salad

SERVES 6 • **PREP TIME:** 10 MINUTES • **COOK TIME:** 9 HOURS
Super Quick Prep

Flank steak has a wonderfully intense, beefy flavor, but it can be a bit tough since it is cut from the bottom abdominal area of the cow, where the muscles do a lot of hard work. However, tough cuts mellow perfectly in the slow cooker. Flank steak also shreds nicely after it's spent the day simmering, so it makes a perfect salad topper. Use the juices from the beef to dress the salad, and feel free to add your favorite chopped-up raw vegetables.

2 teaspoons freshly ground black pepper

1 teaspoon smoked paprika

1 teaspoon garlic powder

½ teaspoon ground coriander

½ teaspoon sea salt

⅛ teaspoon cayenne pepper

1 pound flank steak

2 red bell peppers, seeded and thinly sliced

1 cup Beef Broth (page 30), or store bought

8 cups shredded iceberg lettuce

1. In a small bowl, mix the black pepper, paprika, garlic powder, coriander, salt, and cayenne.

2. Spread the mixture evenly over the flank steak, rubbing it in.

3. In the slow cooker, combine the seasoned flank steak, bell peppers, and broth.

4. Cover and cook on low for 8 hours.

5. Remove the beef from the sauce and shred it with two forks.

6. Return the beef to the sauce and mix well.

7. Serve the shredded beef on top of the shredded lettuce, with the sauce drizzled over the top.

LEFTOVERS TIP This beef is excellent rolled up in whole-wheat tortillas with vegetables, low-fat mayonnaise, and whole-grain mustard for a hearty next-day lunch.

PER SERVING Calories: 180; Total Fat: 7g; Saturated Fat: 3g; Cholesterol: 42mg; Carbohydrates: 6g; Fiber: 2g; Protein: 23g; Sodium: 204mg; Potassium: 465mg

Beef Tacos

SERVES 8 • **PREP TIME:** 10 MINUTES • **COOK TIME:** 8 HOURS
Super Quick Prep

While this taco recipe calls for soft corn tortillas, you can also use whole-wheat tortillas or even make a "naked taco" by spooning the beef and toppings over cooked Brown Rice (page 31). Feel free to add your own favorite toppings and vegetables to make this taco your own recipe.

1½ pounds extra-lean
   ground beef

2 onions, chopped

¼ cup Beef Broth (page 30),
   or store bought

2 tablespoons chili powder

1 teaspoon garlic powder

1 teaspoon ground cumin

1 teaspoon ground coriander

½ teaspoon sea salt

16 soft corn tortillas

½ cup shredded low-fat
   Cheddar cheese

3 tomatoes, chopped

1 cup fat-free sour cream

1. Crumble the ground beef into your slow cooker.
2. Add the onions, broth, chili powder, garlic powder, cumin, coriander, and salt.
3. Cover and cook on low for 8 hours.
4. Break up the beef with a potato masher or a spoon, turning it into small crumbles.
5. Serve on the corn tortillas, topped with Cheddar cheese, tomatoes, and sour cream.

LEFTOVERS TIP If you have leftover taco meat, you can make a quick and easy taco soup with beef broth, canned crushed tomatoes, and vegetables of your choice. Simmer in a pot on the stove top until the vegetables are soft. The taco meat also freezes well in single-serving containers for meals on the go.

PER SERVING Calories: 333; Total Fat: 6g; Saturated Fat: 3g; Cholesterol: 56mg; Carbohydrates: 41g; Fiber: 6g; Protein: 24g; Sodium: 287mg; Potassium: 633mg

Porcupine Meatballs

SERVES 4 • **PREP TIME:** 15 MINUTES • **COOK TIME:** 8 HOURS

These meatballs get their name because the grains of rice within make them look as though they have porcupine quills. To make your meatballs all roughly the same size, use a small ice cream scoop and then just gently pat them into the final shape.

For the sauce

2 (14-ounce) cans diced tomatoes, 1 drained and 1 with its juice

½ onion, grated

3 garlic cloves, minced

1 teaspoon dried Italian seasoning

½ teaspoon sea salt

¼ teaspoon freshly ground black pepper

Pinch cayenne pepper

For the meatballs

1 pound extra-lean ground beef

3 cups cooked Brown Rice (page 31), divided

½ onion, grated

3 garlic cloves, minced

1 egg, beaten

1 teaspoon dried Italian seasoning

½ teaspoon sea salt

¼ teaspoon freshly ground black pepper

To make the sauce

In a medium bowl, mix the tomatoes (including the juice from 1 can), onion, garlic, Italian seasoning, salt, black pepper, and cayenne. Set aside.

To make the meatballs

1. In another bowl, mix the ground beef, 1 cup of cooked rice, the onion, garlic, egg, Italian seasoning, salt, and pepper.

2. Form the mixture into balls. Put the meatballs in your slow cooker.

3. Pour the sauce over the meatballs.

4. Cover and cook on low for 8 hours.

5. Spoon the meatballs and sauce over the remaining 2 cups of cooked rice and serve.

LEFTOVERS TIP Double this recipe and use the meatballs and sauce to make a tasty meatball sub, using whole-wheat rolls and topping it with a little grated low-fat Parmesan cheese.

PER SERVING Calories: 476; Total Fat: 8g; Saturated Fat: 3g; Cholesterol: 103mg; Carbohydrates: 67g; Fiber: 6g; Protein: 33g; Sodium: 573mg; Potassium: 1197mg

Pasta Bolognese

SERVES 6 • **PREP TIME:** 15 MINUTES • **COOK TIME:** 8 HOURS

Bolognese is a traditional Italian meat sauce, typically made with ground veal. If you wish, you can substitute extra-lean ground beef, ground turkey, ground chicken, or even ground pork from a lean cut, such as center loin. Or try a mixture! Bolognese is perfect for the slow cooker, because it is a long-simmered sauce that develops better flavor the longer it cooks. Try using the sauce to top spaghetti squash, which makes a delicious pasta substitute.

1 pound ground veal

3 carrots, peeled and
   finely chopped

2 onions, finely chopped

1 cup dry red wine

1 cup skim milk

2 tablespoons tomato paste

2 teaspoons garlic powder

2 teaspoons Italian seasoning

½ teaspoon sea salt

¼ teaspoon freshly ground
   black pepper

3 cups cooked
   whole-wheat pasta

1. Crumble the ground veal into your slow cooker.

2. Add the carrots, onions, wine, skim milk, tomato paste, garlic powder, Italian seasoning, salt, and pepper.

3. Cover and cook on low for 8 hours.

4. Serve on top of the hot, cooked pasta.

PER SERVING Calories: 322; Total Fat: 7g; Saturated Fat: 2g; Cholesterol: 80mg; Carbohydrates: 32g; Fiber: 4g; Protein: 24g; Sodium: 275mg; Potassium: 600mg

Mustard & Herb Pork Tenderloin

SERVES 4 • **PREP TIME:** 10 MINUTES • **COOK TIME:** 8 HOURS
Super Quick Prep

Pork tenderloin generally isn't ideal for the slow cooker, because it is so lean. However, if you add enough liquid, the meat will stay moist and the flavor of the braising liquid will season the pork as it cooks. In this recipe, the braising liquid includes mustard and herbs that pair perfectly with pork.

1 pound pork tenderloin

1 cup dry white wine

1 cup Poultry Broth (page 29), or store bought

3 tablespoons Dijon mustard

1 tablespoon cornstarch

1 teaspoon dried rosemary

1 teaspoon dried thyme

1 teaspoon dried marjoram

1 teaspoon garlic powder

¼ teaspoon sea salt

¼ teaspoon freshly ground black pepper

1. Put the tenderloin in your slow cooker.

2. In a small bowl, whisk together all the remaining ingredients. Pour the mixture into the slow cooker.

3. Cover and cook on low for 8 hours.

4. Slice the tenderloin and serve with the sauce spooned over the top.

A BALANCED MEAL For a full one-pot meal, add 4 chopped carrots, 1 chopped onion, and 1 pound quartered new potatoes to the slow cooker with the pork and sauce.

PER SERVING Calories: 233; Total Fat: 5g; Saturated Fat: 1g; Cholesterol: 83mg; Carbohydrates: 5g; Fiber: 1g; Protein: 31g; Sodium: 318mg; Potassium: 569mg

Pork Chili Verde

SERVES 8 • **PREP TIME:** 10 MINUTES • **COOK TIME:** 8 HOURS
Super Quick Prep

Pork shoulder is a pretty fatty cut of meat, but you can make it leaner by trimming all the visible fat from the pork cubes before adding them to the pot. This chili verde is nicely spicy, but not over-the-top hot. Using canned diced jalapeños makes prep super easy, because you don't need to spend a lot of time chopping.

2 pounds pork shoulder, trimmed of excess fat and cut into 1-inch cubes

2 onions, chopped

3 (4-ounce) cans diced jalapeño peppers, with their juice

2 cups Poultry Broth (page 29), or store bought

1 teaspoon garlic powder

1 teaspoon ground cumin

½ teaspoon sea salt

¼ teaspoon freshly ground black pepper

Pinch cayenne pepper

1. In your slow cooker, combine all the ingredients.

2. Cover and cook on low for 8 hours.

3. Skim any fat from the top and discard.

PER SERVING Calories: 357; Total Fat: 25g; Saturated Fat: 9g; Cholesterol: 102mg; Carbohydrates: 5g; Fiber: 2g; Protein: 28g; Sodium: 906mg; Potassium: 505mg

Greek Spiced Leg of Lamb

SERVES 8 • **PREP TIME:** 15 MINUTES • **COOK TIME:** 8 HOURS

Leg of lamb tends to be fairly fatty, so it's important to trim all visible fat before you cook it. Since this recipe doesn't use the sauce—just the lamb—a lot of the fat will drain away to the bottom of the slow cooker, where you can toss it out. Serve the sliced lamb on seasoned couscous or pita bread, topped with plain fat-free yogurt and sliced cucumber.

2 teaspoons dried oregano

1 teaspoon dried thyme

1 teaspoon onion powder

1 teaspoon garlic powder

½ teaspoon dried marjoram

½ teaspoon ground cinnamon

½ teaspoon ground nutmeg

½ teaspoon sea salt

¼ teaspoon freshly ground black pepper

1 (2-pound) boneless leg of lamb, butterflied

1 cup Beef Broth (page 30), or store bought

1. In a small bowl, mix the oregano, thyme, onion powder, garlic powder, marjoram, cinnamon, nutmeg, salt, and pepper. Rub the mixture all over the lamb.

2. Put the lamb in the slow cooker and pour the broth over.

3. Cover and cook on low for 8 hours. Slice the lamb and serve.

SMART SHOPPING TIP If you've never butterflied a leg of lamb before, ask your butcher to do it for you. Save the bone to make broth.

PER SERVING Calories: 218; Total Fat: 8g; Saturated Fat: 3g; Cholesterol: 102mg; Carbohydrates: 1g; Fiber: 0g; Protein: 32g; Sodium: 204mg; Potassium: 397mg

Side Dishes & Appetizers

Barbecue Beans

SERVES 8 • **PREP TIME:** 15 MINUTES • **COOK TIME:** 8 HOURS

These slow-cooked beans are savory and sweet and contain a lot less sodium and sugar than baked beans from a can. They also freeze well, so you can put them in single-serving containers and thaw them as needed. Liquid smoke creates the smoky barbecue flavor, while blackstrap molasses provides a dark sweetness that goes perfectly with the spice in these beans. Go ahead and mix up the types of beans for more of a taste variety.

5 cups cooked pinto beans (page 34), rinsed

1 onion, finely chopped

6 garlic cloves, minced

3 jalapeño peppers, seeded and finely chopped

1 (14-ounce) can tomato sauce

¼ cup blackstrap molasses

½ teaspoon liquid smoke

2 teaspoons smoked paprika

¼ teaspoon sea salt

⅛ teaspoon cayenne pepper

1. In your slow cooker, combine all the ingredients.

2. Cover and cook on low for 8 hours.

PER SERVING Calories: 207; Total Fat: 1g; Saturated Fat: 0g; Cholesterol: 0mg; Carbohydrates: 41g; Fiber: 11g; Protein: 11g; Sodium: 467mg; Potassium: 2052mg

PRECOOKING TIP To really distribute the flavor of the onion and peppers throughout the beans, pulse the onion, jalapeños, and garlic in a food processor until they are finely chopped, then add them to the other ingredients in the slow cooker.

"Baked" Sweet Potatoes

SERVES 4 • **PREP TIME:** 5 MINUTES • **COOK TIME:** 8 HOURS
Super Quick Prep

Sweet potatoes make a perfect side dish, particularly when you top them with fat-free sour cream, crumbled turkey bacon, salsa, chopped nuts, or whatever else you like. These potatoes are super easy to make and require almost no preparation.

4 medium sweet potatoes,
  scrubbed

1. Wrap each sweet potato in aluminum foil and put them in the slow cooker.

2. Cover and cook on low for 8 hours.

3. Unwrap to serve.

A BALANCED MEAL Try topping the sweet potatoes with one of the chili recipes in this cookbook for a hearty, balanced meal.

PER SERVING Calories: 112; Total Fat: 0g; Saturated Fat: 0g; Cholesterol: 0mg; Carbohydrates: 26g; Fiber: 4g; Protein: 3g; Sodium: 14mg; Potassium: 1224mg

Spaghetti Squash

SERVES 6 • **PREP TIME:** 10 MINUTES • **COOK TIME:** 8 HOURS
Super Quick Prep

Spaghetti squash is delicious by itself with a little seasoning, or it makes a great pasta replacement for all kinds of dishes. True to its name, spaghetti squash turns into spaghetti-like noodles when you scrape a fork across the cooked flesh. It's a great way to add extra vegetables to your meals, or makes for a tasty snack when drizzled with olive oil and a little low-fat Parmesan.

1 spaghetti squash

¼ cup water

¼ cup olive oil

2 garlic cloves, minced

¼ cup low-fat grated Parmesan cheese

1. Prick the spaghetti squash all over with a fork.

2. Put the squash in the slow cooker and add the water.

3. Cover and cook on low for 8 hours.

4. Allow the squash to cool slightly. When it is cool enough to handle, cut the squash in half.

5. Scrape a fork across the squash flesh to make strands.

6. In a small sauté pan on the stove top, heat the olive oil on medium-high.

7. Add the garlic and cook for 30 seconds.

8. Toss the spaghetti squash with the garlic and olive oil mixture and the Parmesan cheese.

A BALANCED MEAL Toss the spaghetti squash with the Pasta Bolognese Sauce (page 124).

PER SERVING Calories: 128; Total Fat: 10g; Saturated Fat: 2g; Cholesterol: 4mg; Carbohydrates: 10g; Fiber: 0g; Protein: 2g; Sodium: 61mg; Potassium: 113mg

Sweet & Sour Turkey Meatballs

SERVES 6 • **PREP TIME:** 15 MINUTES • **COOK TIME:** 8 HOURS

These meatballs are great to take to a potluck, serve as an appetizer, or dish up on game day. The sweet and sour sauce keeps the turkey moist as it cooks, so there's no need to add extra fat. Feel free to substitute ground chicken or extra-lean beef—either will work equally well.

1 pound ground turkey breast

½ cup whole-wheat
    bread crumbs

1 onion, grated

1 egg, beaten

1 teaspoon sea salt, divided

¼ teaspoon freshly ground
    black pepper

1 (8-ounce) can pineapple
    chunks (no sugar added),
    with its juice

¼ cup apple cider vinegar

2 tablespoons honey

1 tablespoon cornstarch

1. In a medium bowl, mix the ground turkey, bread crumbs, onion, egg, ½ teaspoon of salt, and the pepper.

2. Use a small scoop to form the mixture into meatballs. Put the meatballs in your slow cooker.

3. In a small bowl, whisk together the juice from the canned pineapple (reserve the pineapple chunks), vinegar, honey, cornstarch, and remaining ½ teaspoon of salt.

4. Add the mixture to the slow cooker, then add the pineapple chunks.

5. Cover and cook on low for 8 hours.

PRECOOKING TIP For a richer flavor, brown the meatballs in 2 tablespoons olive oil for 5 to 7 minutes before adding them to the slow cooker.

PER SERVING Calories: 217; Total Fat: 7g; Saturated Fat: 2g; Cholesterol: 83mg; Carbohydrates: 16g; Fiber: 1g; Protein: 23g; Sodium: 438mg; Potassium: 325mg

Asian Meatballs

SERVES 6 • **PREP TIME:** 15 MINUTES • **COOK TIME:** 8 HOURS

Ginger, soy sauce, garlic, and scallions give these meatballs an Asian flavor. They're great as a snack, but they also make a fabulous main dish when served with cooked Brown Rice (page 31) and a stir-fry of your favorite vegetables such as broccoli, bok choy, shiitake mushrooms, pea pods, and carrots.

1 pound ground turkey

6 garlic cloves, minced

6 scallions, minced

1 tablespoon grated fresh ginger

¼ cup chopped fresh cilantro

1 egg, beaten

2 tablespoons low-sodium soy sauce

½ teaspoon sesame-chili oil

¼ cup Poultry Broth (page 29), or store bought

1. In a medium bowl, combine the ground turkey, garlic, scallions, ginger, cilantro, egg, soy sauce, and sesame-chili oil until well mixed.

2. Using a small scoop, form the mixture into balls. Put the meatballs in the slow cooker. Add the broth.

3. Cover and cook on low for 8 hours.

LEFTOVERS TIP To make a delicious Asian meatball soup, simmer the leftover meatballs in Poultry Broth (page 29) with cooked Brown Rice (page 31) and an assortment of sliced or shredded vegetables such as carrots, mushrooms, cabbage, and pea pods.

PER SERVING Calories: 176; Total Fat: 10g; Saturated Fat: 2g; Cholesterol: 104mg; Carbohydrates: 3g; Fiber: 1g; Protein: 23g; Sodium: 388mg; Potassium: 283mg

Hot Wings

SERVES 6 • **PREP TIME:** 10 MINUTES • **COOK TIME:** 8 HOURS
Super Quick Prep

Hot wings make a great snack. Paired with a salad or other side dishes, they're also a tasty meal. Just before it's time to eat, you can whisk up this simple blue cheese dip, or use your favorite fat-free ranch dressing.

1 cup Louisiana hot sauce

2 tablespoons olive oil

½ teaspoon cayenne pepper

2 pounds chicken wings

¼ cup fat-free sour cream

¼ cup fat-free mayonnaise

¼ cup blue cheese crumbles

1 tablespoon Dijon mustard

1 teaspoon low-sodium Worcestershire sauce

3 celery stalks, cut into sticks

1. In a small bowl, whisk together the hot sauce, olive oil, and cayenne. Pour the mixture into the slow cooker.

2. Add the chicken wings and toss to coat.

3. Cover and cook on low for 8 hours.

4. In a small bowl, whisk together the sour cream, mayonnaise, blue cheese crumbles, Dijon mustard, and Worcestershire sauce.

5. Serve the wings and celery sticks with the blue cheese mixture on the side for dipping.

PRECOOKING TIP For even better flavor, brown the chicken wings in 2 tablespoons olive oil for 3 to 5 minutes per side before tossing them into the slow cooker.

PER SERVING Calories: 401; Total Fat: 21g; Saturated Fat: 5g; Cholesterol: 144mg; Carbohydrates: 6g; Fiber: 0g; Protein: 45g; Sodium: 1335mg; Potassium: 452mg

Honey-Soy Chicken Wings

SERVES 6 • **PREP TIME:** 5 MINUTES • **COOK TIME:** 8 HOURS
Super Quick Prep

These sweet, sticky wings are the perfect snack, although you'll need to serve them with lots of napkins since the sauce has a tendency to migrate from wings to fingers. For an attractive party presentation, put them on a platter and sprinkle them with sesame seeds and chopped scallions.

¼ cup honey

¼ cup low-sodium soy sauce

Juice of 1 orange

1 tablespoon grated
  fresh ginger

1 teaspoon garlic powder

2 pounds chicken wings

1 teaspoon sesame seeds

3 scallions, thinly sliced

1. In a small bowl, whisk together the honey, soy sauce, orange juice, ginger, and garlic powder.

2. Put the chicken wings in your slow cooker. Pour the sauce over the wings and stir to coat.

3. Cover and cook on low for 8 hours.

4. Serve garnished with the sesame seeds and scallions.

PER SERVING Calories: 344; Total Fat: 12g; Saturated Fat: 3g; Cholesterol: 135mg; Carbohydrates: 14g; Fiber: 0g; Protein: 45g; Sodium: 719mg; Potassium: 415mg

Spiced Nuts

SERVES 6 • **PREP TIME:** 5 MINUTES • **COOK TIME:** 4 HOURS

Super Quick Prep

These sweet and spicy nuts are loaded with healthy fats, and just a few nuts are enough to satisfy your hungriest snack cravings. Feel free to mix it up with spices (except additional salt) to create your own versions.

Nonstick cooking spray

2 tablespoons honey

1 tablespoon olive oil

Zest of 1 orange

1 teaspoon ground cinnamon

½ teaspoon ground ginger

¼ teaspoon ground nutmeg

½ teaspoon sea salt

⅛ teaspoon cayenne pepper

1 cup unsalted raw pecans
(or other raw nuts of
your choice)

1. Spray the crock of your slow cooker with nonstick cooking spray.

2. In a small bowl, whisk together the honey, olive oil, orange zest, cinnamon, ginger, nutmeg, sea salt, and cayenne.

3. Add the nuts to the slow cooker. Pour the spice mixture over the top.

4. Cover and cook on low for 4 hours.

5. Turn off the slow cooker. Uncover and allow the nuts to cool and harden for 2 hours, stirring occasionally to keep the nuts coated.

PER SERVING Calories: 125; Total Fat: 11g; Saturated Fat: 1g; Cholesterol: 0mg; Carbohydrates: 8g; Fiber: 2g; Protein: 1g; Sodium: 157mg; Potassium: 117mg

French Onion Dip

MAKES 2 CUPS • **PREP TIME:** 10 MINUTES • **COOK TIME:** 10 HOURS
Super Quick Prep

To make this dip, you caramelize thinly sliced onions in your slow cooker first, and then mix them into the other ingredients. The tasty result is low in salt and is delicious served as a topping for the "Baked" Sweet Potatoes (page 131), or you can use it as a dip for bell pepper, carrot, and celery sticks.

3 onions, thinly sliced

3 tablespoons olive oil

1 teaspoon dried thyme

½ teaspoon sea salt

⅛ teaspoon freshly ground black pepper

¾ cup fat-free sour cream

¾ cup fat-free cream cheese, softened

Pinch cayenne pepper

1. In your slow cooker, toss the onions with the olive oil, thyme, salt, and pepper.

2. Cover and cook on low for 8 hours.

3. Remove the lid. Turn the slow cooker to high. Continue cooking, stirring occasionally, until the liquid nearly evaporates, 1 to 2 hours. Allow the onions to cool for 1 hour.

4. In a small bowl, beat together the sour cream, cream cheese, and cayenne (a hand mixer works well for this).

5. Stir in the onions and serve.

PER SERVING (¼ CUP) Calories: 160; Total Fat: 13g; Saturated Fat: 6g; Cholesterol: 26mg; Carbohydrates: 8g; Fiber: 1g; Protein: 3g; Sodium: 202mg; Potassium: 88mg

Spinach and Artichoke Dip

MAKES 1½ CUPS • **PREP TIME:** 10 MINUTES • **COOK TIME:** 4 HOURS
Super Quick Prep

This artichoke dip cooks quickly on low, so it's best to make it on a weekend when you're home. It's a delicious game day or party snack, and if you're making it for a crowd, you can serve it directly from the slow cooker. Use whole-grain crackers and sliced carrots, bell peppers, celery, and jicama for dipping. It also makes a tasty topping for meat or potatoes.

2 (14-ounce) cans artichoke hearts, drained and chopped

2 cups baby spinach, stemmed

½ red onion, minced

3 garlic cloves, minced

8 ounces fat-free cream cheese

2 cups fat-free sour cream

Zest of 1 lemon

¼ teaspoon sea salt

¼ teaspoon freshly ground black pepper

Pinch cayenne pepper

1. In your slow cooker, combine all the ingredients.

2. Cover and cook on low for 4 hours.

PER SERVING (¼ CUP) Calories: 283; Total Fat: 13g; Saturated Fat: 8g; Cholesterol: 50mg; Carbohydrates: 30g; Fiber: 7g; Protein: 10g; Sodium: 390mg; Potassium: 612mg

Desserts & Treats

Maple-Ginger Applesauce

SERVES 6 • **PREP TIME:** 15 MINUTES • **COOK TIME:** 8 HOURS

Peeling, coring, and chopping apples can be a bit time-consuming, unless you have a handy tool called an apple peeler-corer. It looks like a vice and screws onto your countertop. You turn the handle and the apple comes out perfectly peeled, cored, and sliced. While it's not essential, if you cook with a lot of apples (and why wouldn't you?), it's a real time-saver.

3 sweet-tart red apples (such as Pink Lady or Honeycrisp), peeled, cored, and sliced

3 tart green apples (such as Granny Smith), peeled, cored, and sliced

1 tablespoon grated fresh ginger

Juice of ½ lemon

½ cup pure maple syrup

¼ cup water

1 teaspoon ground cinnamon

Pinch sea salt

1. In your slow cooker, combine all the ingredients.

2. Cover and cook on low for 8 hours.

3. For a smoother applesauce, strain through a sieve or food mill, or process in the food processor or blender.

LEFTOVERS TIP Applesauce goes perfectly with pork and chicken, so it makes a tasty side dish or sauce for a simply cooked pork tenderloin or chicken breast.

PER SERVING Calories: 167; Total Fat: 0g; Saturated Fat: 0g; Cholesterol: 0mg; Carbohydrates: 44g; Fiber: 5g; Protein: 1g; Sodium: 43mg; Potassium: 262mg

Baked Five-Spice Apples

SERVES 4 • **PREP TIME:** 15 MINUTES • **COOK TIME:** 8 HOURS

To prepare the apples for this dish, leave the peel on. Slice off the top with a sharp knife and scoop out the core with a small spoon, leaving the bottom of the apple intact. This leaves a hole in the center of the apple, into which you can stuff all kinds of tasty fillings.

¼ cup honey

Zest and juice of 1 orange

1½ teaspoons Chinese five-spice powder

3 tablespoons chopped pecans

4 sweet-tart apples, cored, bottoms intact

1. In a small bowl, whisk together the honey, orange zest (reserve the juice), and five-spice powder. Add the pecans and stir to coat.

2. Spoon the mixture evenly into the cavities created in the apples.

3. Stand the apples up in your slow cooker.

4. Pour the reserved orange juice over the top of the apples.

5. Cover and cook on low for 8 hours.

PER SERVING Calories: 232; Total Fat: 8g; Saturated Fat: 1g; Cholesterol: 0mg; Carbohydrates: 44g; Fiber: 6g; Protein: 2g; Sodium: 3mg; Potassium: 236mg

Bourbon Peaches

SERVES 6 • **PREP TIME:** 10 MINUTES • **COOK TIME:** 8 HOURS
Super Quick Prep

Boozy peaches make a delicious dessert by themselves, or they are tasty as a topping for pudding (such as the Rice Pudding on page 148) or low-fat ice cream. Although you don't need to buy top-shelf bourbon for this recipe, do choose a decent brand, because the taste of the booze will affect the final flavor of the dish.

6 peaches, peeled, pitted, and cut into quarters

¼ cup chopped walnuts

¼ cup bourbon

¼ cup pure maple syrup

½ teaspoon ground cinnamon

1. In your slow cooker, combine all the ingredients.

2. Cover and cook on low for 8 hours.

PER SERVING Calories: 127; Total Fat: 3g; Saturated Fat: 0g; Cholesterol: 0mg; Carbohydrates: 19g; Fiber: 2g; Protein: 2g; Sodium: 1mg; Potassium: 241mg

PRECOOKING TIP Give the walnuts more flavor by lightly toasting them before adding them to the slow cooker. To do this, put them in a dry sauté pan and put it on the stove top on medium-high. Cook the walnuts, stirring constantly, until fragrant, about 3 minutes.

Honey & Fennel Pears

SERVES 6 • **PREP TIME:** 10 MINUTES • **COOK TIME:** 8 HOURS
Super Quick Prep

Fennel seed, with its light licorice flavor, is the perfect accompaniment for pears. These pears wind up quite soft, so stirring in toasted hazelnuts at the end adds a bit of crunch to the texture. You can eat these pears alone, use them as a topping for pancakes and waffles, or enjoy them with a scoop of low-fat ice cream.

6 pears, peeled, halved, and cored

Juice and zest of 1 orange

¼ cup honey

1½ teaspoons ground fennel seed

½ teaspoon ground cinnamon

Pinch ground nutmeg

Pinch sea salt

¼ cup chopped hazelnuts

1. In your slow cooker, arrange the pears cut-side up.
2. In a small bowl, whisk together the orange juice and zest, honey, fennel seed, cinnamon, nutmeg, and salt. Pour the mixture evenly over the pears.
3. Cover and cook on low for 8 hours.
4. In a small sauté pan, cook the hazelnuts on medium-heat, stirring constantly, until fragrant, 3 to 5 minutes.
5. Sprinkle the hazelnuts over the pears and serve.

PER SERVING Calories: 186; Total Fat: 2g; Saturated Fat: 0g; Cholesterol: 0mg; Carbohydrates: 44g; Fiber: 7g; Protein: 1g; Sodium: 43mg; Potassium: 281mg

Orange-Cranberry Compote

SERVES 6 • **PREP TIME:** 10 MINUTES • **COOK TIME:** 8 HOURS
Super Quick Prep

The flavor combination of oranges and cranberries is a classic. Cranberries are naturally tart, while oranges are sweet and add a nice note of citrus and brightness. Chopped fennel is a surprising addition to this lightly sweet compote, adding a hint of licorice. For texture, stir in chopped toasted pecans just before serving.

12 ounces fresh or
  frozen cranberries

1 fennel bulb, chopped

Zest of 1 orange

Juice of 2 oranges

¼ cup honey

1 teaspoon ground ginger

½ teaspoon cinnamon

Pinch sea salt

¼ cup chopped pecans

1. In your slow cooker, combine the cranberries, fennel, orange zest, orange juice, honey, ginger, cinnamon, and salt.

2. Cover and cook on low for 8 hours.

3. In a small sauté pan, heat the pecans on medium, stirring constantly, until fragrant, 3 to 5 minutes.

4. Stir the pecans into the cranberry compote.

LEFTOVERS TIP Pep up your breakfast oatmeal by topping it with ¼ cup of this tasty cranberry compote.

PER SERVING Calories: 122; Total Fat: 4g; Saturated Fat: 0g; Cholesterol: 0mg; Carbohydrates: 21g; Fiber: 4g; Protein: 1g; Sodium: 60mg; Potassium: 297mg

Maple Banana Sundaes

SERVES 6 • **PREP TIME:** 10 MINUTES • **COOK TIME:** 2 HOURS
Super Quick Prep

This recipe uses some of the flavors of bananas Foster without the flambé or all the butter. It's served with fat-free ice cream or frozen yogurt, or you can just eat the bananas by themselves. This recipe is best when just made, and it takes only a couple of hours, so you can plan it as a nice surprise after a meal.

Nonstick cooking spray

4 bananas, peeled, halved crosswise, and then halved lengthwise

2 tablespoons chopped unsalted pecans

½ cup pure maple syrup

1 teaspoon rum extract

1 tablespoon unsalted butter, melted

Zest and juice of 1 orange

Pinch sea salt

6 scoops low-fat vanilla ice cream or frozen yogurt

1. Spray the crock of your slow cooker with nonstick cooking spray.

2. Put the bananas and unsalted pecans in the bottom of the crock.

3. In a small bowl, whisk together the maple syrup, rum extract, butter, orange zest and juice, and salt. Pour the syrup mixture over the bananas and pecans.

4. Cover and cook on low for 2 hours.

5. To serve, spoon the bananas, pecans, and syrup over the ice cream.

PER SERVING Calories: 368; Total Fat: 15g; Saturated Fat: 8g; Cholesterol: 47mg; Carbohydrates: 59g; Fiber: 3g; Protein: 5g; Sodium: 113mg; Potassium: 493mg

Rice Pudding

SERVES 6 • **PREP TIME:** 10 MINUTES • **COOK TIME:** 8 HOURS
Super Quick Prep

This creamy rice pudding uses brown rice, so it has fiber as well as flavor. Fragrantly spiced with cinnamon and filled with dried fruit, it is a delicious dessert that doesn't take much prep time but yields spectacular results. For the finest flavor, use the best vanilla extract you can.

⅔ cup uncooked brown rice

½ cup dried fruit of your choice, such as raisins, cranberries, apples, or a mixture

1 (13-ounce) can light coconut milk

1½ cups skim milk

¼ cup honey

1 teaspoon pure vanilla extract

1 teaspoon ground cinnamon

¼ teaspoon ground nutmeg

Pinch sea salt

1. In your slow cooker, combine all the ingredients.

2. Cover and cook on low for 8 hours.

PER SERVING Calories: 332; Total Fat: 15g; Saturated Fat: 13g; Cholesterol: 1mg; Carbohydrates: 46g; Fiber: 3g; Protein: 6g; Sodium: 84mg; Potassium: 413mg

Mexican Hot Chocolate

SERVES 6 • **PREP TIME:** 5 MINUTES • **COOK TIME:** 4 HOURS
Super Quick Prep

This is a great sweet drink to keep on low in your slow cooker all day when you're having a family gathering. That way, your guests can dip into the hot chocolate whenever they want. The recipe doubles and triples well, so it's easy to have it available for as many people as you wish.

6 ounces bittersweet chocolate, chopped

3 cups skim milk

¼ cup pure maple syrup

½ teaspoon pure vanilla extract

¼ teaspoon ground cinnamon

Pinch sea salt

Pinch cayenne pepper

1. In your slow cooker, combine all the ingredients.
2. Cover and cook on low, whisking occasionally as the chocolate melts, for 4 hours. Serve immediately or reduce the heat to keep warm to serve throughout the day.

LEFTOVERS TIP There's no need to throw away any leftover beverage. Refrigerate it for up to 3 days and reheat, or pour it into ice pop molds for a tasty frozen treat.

PER SERVING Calories: 232; Total Fat: 8g; Saturated Fat: 6g; Cholesterol: 9mg; Carbohydrates: 32g; Fiber: 1g; Protein: 6g; Sodium: 128mg; Potassium: 324mg

The Dirty Dozen
& the Clean Fifteen

A nonprofit and environmental watchdog organization called the Environmental Working Group (EWG) looks at data supplied by the US Department of Agriculture (USDA) and the Food and Drug Administration (FDA) about pesticide residues. Each year it compiles a list of the lowest and highest pesticide loads found in commercial crops. You can use these lists to decide which fruits and vegetables to buy organic to minimize your exposure to pesticides and which produce is considered safe enough to buy conventionally. This does not mean they are pesticide-free, though, so wash these fruits and vegetables thoroughly.

These lists change every year, so make sure you look up the most recent one before you fill your shopping cart. You'll find the most recent lists as well as a guide to pesticides in produce at EWG.org/FoodNews.

The Dirty Dozen*

- » Apples
- » Celery
- » Cherry tomatoes
- » Cucumbers
- » Grapes
- » Nectarines (imported)
- » Peaches
- » Potatoes
- » Snap peas (imported)
- » Spinach
- » Strawberries
- » Sweet bell peppers

* Kale/Collard greens & Hot peppers

The Clean Fifteen

- » Asparagus
- » Avocados
- » Cabbage
- » Cantaloupes (domestic)
- » Cauliflower
- » Eggplants
- » Grapefruits
- » Kiwis
- » Mangos
- » Onions
- » Papayas
- » Pineapples
- » Sweet corn
- » Sweet peas (frozen)
- » Sweet potatoes

* In addition to the dirty dozen, the EWG added two produce contaminated with highly toxic organo-phosphate insecticides.

Measurement Conversion Tables

VOLUME EQUIVALENTS (LIQUID)

US Standard	US Standard (ounces)	Metric (approximate)
2 tablespoons	1 fl. oz.	30 mL
¼ cup	2 fl. oz.	60 mL
½ cup	4 fl. oz.	120 mL
1 cup	8 fl. oz.	240 mL
1½ cups	12 fl. oz.	355 mL
2 cups or 1 pint	16 fl. oz.	475 mL
4 cups or 1 quart	32 fl. oz.	1 L
1 gallon	128 fl. oz.	4 L

OVEN TEMPERATURES

Fahrenheit (F)	Celsius (C) (approximate)
250°F	120°C
300°F	150°C
325°F	165°C
350°F	180°C
375°F	190°C
400°F	200°C
425°F	220°C
450°F	230°C

VOLUME EQUIVALENTS (DRY)

US Standard	Metric (approximate)
¼ teaspoon	1 mL
½ teaspoon	2 mL
1 teaspoon	5 mL
1 tablespoon	15 mL
¼ cup	59 mL
⅓ cup	79 mL
½ cup	118 mL
1 cup	177 mL

WEIGHT EQUIVALENTS

US Standard	Metric (approximate)
½ ounce	15 g
1 ounce	30 g
2 ounces	60 g
4 ounces	115 g
8 ounces	225 g
12 ounces	340 g
16 ounces or 1 pound	455 g

References

Blumenthal, James A., Michael A. Babyak, Alan Hinderliter, Lana L. Watkins, Linda Craighead, Pao-Hwa Lin, Carla Caccia, Julie Johnson, Robert Waugh, and Andrew Sherwood. "Effects of the DASH Diet Alone and in Combination with Exercise and Weight Loss on Blood Pressure and Cardiovascular Biomarkers in Men and Women with High Blood Pressure: The ENCORE Study." *Archives of Internal Medicine* 170, no. 2 (2010): 126. doi:10.1001/archinternmed.2009.470.

Mayo Clinic Staff. "DASH Diet: Healthy Eating to Lower Your Blood Pressure." MayoClinic.org. May 15, 2013. www.mayoclinic.org/healthy-lifestyle/nutrition-and-healthy-eating/in-depth /dash-diet/art-20048456.

Mayo Clinic Staff. "Sample Menus for the DASH Diet." MayoClinic.org. April 10, 2015. www.mayoclinic.org/healthy-lifestyle/nutrition-and-healthy-eating/in-depth/dash-diet /art-20047110.

Obarzanek, Eva, Frank M. Sacks, William M. Vollmer, George A. Bray, Edgar R. Miller, Pao-Hwa Lin, Njeri M. Karanja, et al. "Effects on Blood Lipids of a Blood Pressure–Lowering Diet: The Dietary Approaches to Stop Hypertension (DASH) Trial." *American Journal of Clinical Nutrition* 74, no. 1 (2001): 80–89.

USDA Food Safety and Inspection Service. "Slow Cookers and Food Safety." February 2012. www.fsis.usda.gov/shared/PDF/Slow_Cookers_and_Food_Safety.pdf.

Recipe Index

Index

CPSIA information can be obtained
at www.ICGtesting.com
Printed in the USA
BVOW10s2029031216
469458BV00001BB/1/P

9 781623 157265